ROBERT BOYERS

F. R. LEAVIS

JUDGMENT AND THE
DISCIPLINE OF THOUGHT

A   LITERARY   FRONTIERS   EDITION

UNIVERSITY   OF   MISSOURI   PRESS

COLUMBIA   &   LONDON,   1978

199016

Research on this study was made possible by a grant from the Mellon Foundation. I wish to express my special thanks to Professor Eric Weller, Dean of Faculty at Skidmore College, who administered the research grant.

Thanks also to Professor Thomas S. W. Lewis of Skidmore College, who read the manuscript and made important corrections.

Library of Congress Cataloging in Publication Data

Boyers, Robert
    F. R. Leavis, judgment and
    the discipline of thought.

    (A Literary frontiers edition)
    Includes bibliographical references.
    1. Leavis, Frank Raymond, 1895–
    2. Criticism—Great Britain.
    3. English literature—History and
    criticism. I. Title.
    PR29.L4B63   801'.95'0924   78–54704

To My Wife Peg—
for judgments scrupulous and mild—
and for Lowell & Zachary Meyer Boyers

INTRODUCTION

IT may be, as George Steiner has written, that "great critics are rarer than great poets or novelists." But what is one to make of such an observation? Not, surely, that it is more difficult to write a great critical essay than a great poem, or that the critical enterprise is in itself exhausting in a way that composing a novel is not. Perhaps we have so few great critics because the best writers and thinkers are rarely content to do sustained critical work, because they inevitably tend to try their hands at other things. Or perhaps we think we have few great critics only because we do not know how to evaluate criticism. No one will dispute the fact that a great poem —rare though it may be—is easier to recognize and appraise than a great critical essay. When we read Yeats's "Sailing to Byzantium," we are encouraged more or less at once to think of Yeats as a great writer much of whose other work will warrant close study. I don't know that it's possible to take comparable encouragement from any one critical essay. Does the best essay by Samuel Johnson or by T. S. Eliot indicate that these men are probably to be ranked as great critics? Maybe, but it is hardly clear that educated readers will agree on the necessary qualities of those essays that so recommend them, and their authors, to our esteem.

The English writer F. R. Leavis has been by all odds the most influential English critic of his generation. In this century, only T. S. Eliot may be said to have shaped opinion and stimulated controversy in a comparable degree. They owe their preeminence to very different factors. Eliot was, first, a great poet whose essays attracted attention both because they performed important critical functions and because they reflected his own interests and resources as a writer. Leavis was, from the first, an audacious polemicist and a judge, an arbiter whose mission was to train a generation in the disciplines of critical thinking. Resistance to him was and has continued to be very considerable. Had he been, like Eliot, a great poet, he would no doubt have had an easier time, but there is no use in lamenting the fact that poets and other "creative" spirits are today taken seriously in a way that can only be envied even by the most accomplished critics. Leavis had his say, in a variety of books and articles published over the course of almost fifty years. He was argued with and vilified and caricatured, but he persisted. He had disciples and a fair share of attention—though not often of a useful or appropriate kind. More and more, in the later stages of his career, Leavis implicitly drew the lines of an imagined battle between himself and Eliot, as though only one could be permitted to stand as the critical voice of the age. Eliot has had the better of this competition, if only because, in refusing to strike open blows and in dying while Leavis was still battering vehemently, he avoided the self-wounding and meanness invariably generated by such combats. We shall have occasion in this study to look into the competition, and to consider the relation between such qualities as meanness and forthrightness in the work of a man like Leavis. But it is only fair to say at once that, whatever their relative merits, both Eliot and Leavis produced important critical studies without which the examination of literature in the United States and in England would today be very different than it is. If Leavis's stature as a great critic is still open to debate, the reason may have more to do with our uncertainty about standards of evaluation than with any radical incapacities in Leavis or his work.

The object of the present study is to discover what it

is that distinguishes Leavis's work from most of what passes for criticism in our time and to try to understand the nature of the judicial function in criticism. In this sense, the book is not so much about Leavis as it is about the enterprise to which he has given his name. It is, if you will, a case study that aims to diagnose the conditions of literary study in our day and to consider how central to civilized intercourse are the disciplines associated with criticism as it has been understood and practiced by Leavis. It is by no means a brief for Leavis's opinions on particular writers or an effort to corroborate his view of contemporary high culture. Throughout, my focus is Leavis only insofar as he engages our attention on issues we can usefully argue by working through his formulations. Everyone who has read even a little Leavis knows that he disapproves of efforts to extend anything he has written from one point to another. His view is that only he can make those extensions, for only he can know exactly what is intended in a given judgment or expository formulation. No matter. Though no one of my acquaintance would wish to apply Leavisian formulations as though they were controlled methodologies or literary keys, it is certainly reasonable to consider what can be done with discriminative procedures developed by an important critic. We want to determine precisely what Leavis has meant by judgment and how useful his discriminative procedures may be in permitting a reader to arrive at sensible judgments of his own. Also, we must consider the problematic relation between authority and the legitimacy of particular "value" judgments. If Leavis has provoked angry response in many quarters, he has done so in part by insisting that there is a basis of living authority from which the various issues can be pronounced upon. In the present moment of our culture, many argue not merely that Leavis has no title to the authority he has claimed as rightfully his but that there is no conceivable basis upon which anyone may legitimately pass binding judgments. The student of criticism, of critical thinking, must confront this issue without supposing that because Leavis has only occasionally acknowledged that it exists, it is marginal to his work. It is central to his thought, as to the thought of other important writers.

In a study such as this one, we must make do with summary statements of biographical information. Ronald Hayman has in any case provided a modest fleshing out of the already familiar facts. His critical biography of Leavis[1] tells us what most of us have long known or picked up from Leavis's intermittent autobiographical digressions deliberately placed in one discourse or another: that Leavis, born in 1895, had a hard time making his way in the Cambridge of the twenties and thirties; that he courted disfavor by openly challenging the views of his professorial colleagues; that his early works were largely ignored by the "serious" reviews of his day; that his marriage to Q.D. (Roth) Leavis in the thirties gave him a helpmate and collaborator whose support was decisive in permitting him to grow and persist in the face of constant hostility; and finally, that his founding of the Cambridge journal *Scrutiny* in 1932 gave him a base of operations from which to launch a whole school of criticism that grew in influence well beyond the demise of the magazine in 1953. Beyond these are the simple facts of Leavis's life as an author: that he and his wife wrote an extraordinary number of articles and reviews for *Scrutiny*, many of which were subsequently collected in the books that made Leavis famous; that he appeared to like nothing better than an opportunity to pick quarrels with "rival" critics, including those he said he admired, like T. S. Eliot, Marius Bewley, and George Santayana; that he early de-

1. See Hayman's *F. R. Leavis* (London: Heinemann, 1976).

4

veloped, and earned, a reputation as a harsh and unrelenting critic who could attack critical opponents with a virulence rarely encountered in the critical writing of our time[2]; that his books *New Bearings in English Poetry* (1932) and *D. H. Lawrence: Novelist* (1955) decisively affected the literate consensus on the state of modern letters; that *Revaluation* (1936) and *The Great Tradition* (1948) established a new and, for some, a highly appealing view of the major poets and novelists in the English tradition—a view, moreover, that serious writers and critics have had to contend with in working out their own accounts of the tradition.[3] On his death at age eighty-two, Leavis was still a center of controversy. From 1965 to 1978 he issued several new books, some reprinting valuable material buried in old issues of *Scrutiny*. The most notable of the newer volumes, coauthored with his wife, is a book on Dickens[4] in which, without any explicit acknowledgment, Leavis drastically adjusts his former perspective and treats Dickens as no reader of his earlier damaging critiques of the novelist could possibly have foreseen. Altogether, a remarkable and somewhat bewildering gesture for a critic who has made much of consistency and wholeness as criteria to which serious critics are inevitably

2. No one should believe that Leavis waited until his old age to become really scathing, that a C. P. Snow was required to bring out the full force of his invective. (See the American edition of *Two Cultures? The Significance of C. P. Snow* [New York: Pantheon, 1963] for Leavis's fullest exposition of the controversy that made him so exceptionally unpopular in English publishing circles in the 1960s.) So decent and honored a scholar as A. C. Bradley could bring on a quite crushing and ironic attack in a much earlier essay, "Diabolic Intellect and the Noble Hero" (reprinted in *The Common Pursuit* [London: Chatto and Windus, 1952]).

3. Often the best recent critics get their bearings by arguing with Leavis, or by using him to support their discoveries. See recent works by Frank Kermode, Donald Davie, John Bayley, George Steiner, among many others.

4. *Dickens The Novelist* (London: Chatto and Windus, 1970).

5

responsive. But there will be much to say of those criteria, and others.

We shall proceed, then, to consider Leavis as the prototype of a certain kind of critic whose commitment to criticism is undivided and, in that sense at least, exemplary. In studying Leavis, we shall confront issues central to criticism as an enterprise, and we shall have a lucid and varied body of work on which to test our understanding of the judicial function as an indispensable activity of thought. The first part of the book will discuss the relevant questions in a fully speculative way, working toward precise formulations of key ideas and principles to which Leavis has shown continued allegiance. In part two, those precise formulations will be called upon for sustained analyses of two novelists and their impact on a critic who has written extensively on their work. These chapters will provide a sustained study in practical criticism, an analysis of the relation between critical predisposition and the literary text. In James and Lawrence we have the variety we need to consider the range and dexterity of Leavis's thought. In evaluating the final significance of his achievement, we hope to have arrived at some plausible and legitimizing account of the critical vocation. That criticism needs legitimizing is an idea that I intend incidentally to enforce.

PART I.

THE OBJECTS OF
CRITICAL THINKING

LEAVIS has been the most difficult of critics to write about. Where other critics have elaborated systems or formal procedures, he has resolutely resisted anything like a consistent approach to literary texts. Though he has returned again and again to particular writers, he has often shifted ground in his treatment of them, leaving us a little uncertain about where to lay final emphasis. There is a litany of judgment terms that, though he will rarely leave it behind for long, is so elusive in the variety of ways in which it is sounded that it is unlikely to reassure anyone not already disposed to take Leavis's judgments on faith. Most important, Leavis has insisted throughout his career that the essential things can rarely be said with the precision we admire. We try to get them said as well as we can; we know that critical language—like poetic language—can be refined and improved by constant practice. But we may not demand what it is positively harmful to demand: that only what can be stated clearly and logically is worthy of belief or acceptance. The critic's business is to participate in a creative reading of texts, which is a way of responding to the common experience as it ought to be apprehended by alert and decently educated persons. Response in this sense is a matter, not primarily of definition, but of evocation. The critic evokes the object or text before him and evokes in an act of re-creation his progressive response to that object. In arriving at a judgment, he judges the quality of life embodied in the given text. In part, this is a judgment on the quality of response invited by the text. The critic considering Milton, or Pope, or Auden, considers as well what they make of him, what they prompt him to require of himself. At his best, Leavis operates in these terms, which is to say, operates with a care and closeness of response that is difficult to generalize.

Here and there, while rejecting theory as the business of criticism, Leavis has done what he could to formulate working principles. These statements have their use, though key designations are often subject in them to shifting emphases. In an early essay on "Literary Criticism and Philosophy,"[1] Leavis responds to René Wellek by stating, "Words in poetry invite us, not to 'think about' and judge but to 'feel into' or 'become'—to realize a complex experience that is given in the words." This kind of "responsiveness," Leavis goes on to argue, "is incompatible with the judicial, one-eye-on-the-standard approach." This is clear enough, insofar as it may be said to constitute a corrective to an overly simple view of criticism that Wellek had mistakenly attributed to Leavis in a 1937 review of *Revaluation*. Leavis does not erect a rigid standard by which to pass judgments on writers who pass before the bar. He insists, always, upon concrete judgments and particular instances. But he ought not to have denied that he characteristically operates from the basis of a standard. In answering Wellek, he leaves himself open to misapprehension by any but the closest and most scrupulous student of his thought. For in Leavis's criticism there is an alertness to standards, and he always responded to "words in poetry" as though they invited him, not merely to " 'feel into' or 'become' " but to judge. In "Luddites? or There is Only One Culture," Leavis speaks of the educated public that makes possible

1. Reprinted in *The Common Pursuit* (London: Chatto & Windus, 1952; Penguin, 1962), pp. 211 ff.

8

standards "for the critic to appeal to."[2] In another essay he quotes with full approval a passage from the philosopher Marjorie Grene, a fragment of which states that "what I have is the power of bringing each new particular to the bar of judgement according to a principle, a standard by which I judge it." That the standard may be said to resist verbal formulation, that it defies " 'clear and logical' statement," is sufficient to make the entire notion acceptable to Leavis.[3] This is fair enough, though the skeptical reader will want some reassurance that he and Leavis are thinking about the same things when they look at words like *judgment* and *standard*. If Leavis can say at one point that judgment crucially matters, at another point that it may not be consistent with the supple responsiveness he admires, he will need to be examined more closely than we have thought necessary in our transactions with other critics.

Looking closely at some of Leavis's designations will necessarily entail an effort of application and definition from which he has tried to warn us away on numerous occasions. There is no help for this. Leavis has taken firm hold of procedures required for his purposes, and we can do no less where our purposes are concerned. What, then, does he propose to do when he judges, and how is it possible to proceed without fixed standards? In an essay called "Approches to T. S. Eliot,"[4] not one of his more memorable studies, Leavis supports Eliot's contention that, "when you judge poetry it is as poetry you must judge it, and not as another thing." This means,

2. Reprinted in *Nor Shall My Sword* (New York: Barnes & Noble, 1972), p. 98.
3. The passages from Marjorie Grene's *The Knower and The Known* are central to Leavis's argument in "Thought, Language and Objectivity" in *The Living Principle* (New York: Oxford, 1975).
4. In *The Common Pursuit*.

one supposes, that a poem must be seen to do something that can only be done by a poem. In this sense, a poem, a successful poem, may not be said to state something in the way that a magazine article will state an opinion or a series of facts. Leavis has made this point on so many occasions that it is useless to refer the reader to any one location. In its various contexts the point seems as clear as anyone might wish. A poem embodies what Leavis calls "the living principle," which is "a concrete some-thing apprehended but indefinable." It does not put ideas into words. It searches out what it wants to get at, using words in a way that is at once creative and unstable. The element of surprise is everywhere present as a possibility that may open up the discourse, inviting the reader to a response that is genuinely collaborative. When we judge the poem, we judge not what it says, but what it is.

Though interesting and, from an educational point of view, salutary, none of this is likely to seem fully help-ful to the occasional reader of Leavis's criticism. His work on Milton is a case in point. That Milton was a very great poet Leavis does not care to deny. Nor does it really mat-ter crucially, for our purposes, what Leavis's estimates of this figure or that happened to be. What matters is that Leavis speaks of Milton in a way that is difficult to square with his commitment to poetry as poetry. In a piece on "The Augustan Tradition and the 18th Century," [5] Leavis rejects one of Eliot's now familiar formulations, that "To have the virtues of good prose is the first and minimum requirement of good poetry." Not so, according to Leavis: though Augustan verse may satisfy "expectations regard-ing order and connectedness that we bring from prose," neither the work of Blake nor of Eliot—nor of most other poets one might name—can satisfy those expectations.

5. *Revaluation* (Stewart, 1936; New York: Norton, 1963), Chapter 4.

When we use terms like *precision of statement*, we know we are not talking about the verse of most of the poets we admire. The *prose attitude of mind* is generally alien to the creation—as to the collaborative reception—of genuine poetry. We do not have to detest faculties of reason and order to know their limitations. If we wish to speak of a poet like Milton, to formulate plausible judgments about him, we must know what we are considering.

How is it, then, that Leavis should think it suitable to say of Milton that he "certainly hasn't the kind of energy of mind for sustained analytic and discursive thinking," that he "is not really interested in the achievement of precise thought"?[6] Is it the business of poetry to provide "sustained analytic and discursive thinking"? Leavis would no doubt have to respond that the business of any poem is to do what it ought to do. In this sense, Milton may be required to think and analyze in a particular way because the project of his own work demands that he do so. The critic doesn't impose these requirements according to some whim of his own. He responds to the poem at hand with the fullness of his own experience. Where he feels some failure, senses the lack of something vital—in the poem as in his own grasp of it—he moves to locate the source of that failure. The act of reading is an act of judgment in the degree in which it insists that things be what they are, that they realize themselves as fully as they ought to. If Milton fails to provide what Leavis asks, the issue is not so much whether Leavis has asked the same things of other poets; the issue is, how just is it to ask Milton that he achieve a precision of thought that may not have been a primary part of his intention.

In fact, Leavis does not examine Milton's work in a way that would support his contentions. Though he has much to say of local texture in *Paradise Lost, Lycidas,* and

6. "Mr. Eliot and Milton" in *The Common Pursuit.*

11

Samson Agonistes, he doesn't challenge the Miltonic project in its generality. When he dismisses the "architectural" dimensions of Milton's work as appealing to minds moved by "inertly orthodox generalities," we are interested, but can in no way be said to yield.[7] The particular judgments lack necessary support and detail in the context that gives them form. Only by going outside the immediate context of those essays on Milton can we find what we need, not necessarily to support, but to explain Leavis's strictures. It is important that we do so, again, not because it matters so very much that Leavis has had unfavorable things to say of Milton but because we can know better what we are about when we see clearly how Leavis operates.

To go outside the immediate context of a given criticism is not always a simple matter. This much we've already begun to see. I cannot conveniently speak of Milton as I might of Pope or Shelley. Leavis has had so much to say of so many figures that one will need to proceed with great caution in relating his strictures on one to his praise of others. What we may appropriately use is best discovered by looking for signs or suggestions in the given context. In the Milton essays a major focus is local texture, understood as something more than a concern for occasional felicity in the verse. As in other items, Eliot's antecedent criticism figures prominently in the organizing of the essays. Particularly interesting to Leavis is Eliot's description of Milton's verse as "magniloquent": "To say that Milton's verse is magniloquent is to say that it is not doing as much as its impressive pomp and volume seem to be asserting." More, "he exhibits a feeling *for* words rather than a capacity to feel *through* words." This is helpful. Leavis, in this instance following Eliot

7. See the conclusion to Leavis's chapter on Milton in *Revaluation.*

rather closely, feels that the verse at hand cannot deliver on its promise. It is full of impressive sounds, it is a gorgeous display, but it has little of the felt life and perceived detail of actual experience that would warrant the brilliance of its effects.

A defender of Milton, like C. S. Lewis, in an account provided by Donald Davie, "says in effect that when Dr. Leavis reads *Paradise Lost*, he refuses to honor the contract proper to the heroic poem; he gives the wrong sort of attention and expects the wrong sort of profit."[8] But Leavis, though not always assiduous to "cover himself" and prevent misreading, knows what he wants in the literature he admires and builds a very subtle argument. The convention of genre, after all, is not enough to ensure that every heroic poem will require the same responses of its readers. What Leavis is after is a quality of genuineness that can only be discovered in the particular engagement with the single text. To ask that impressive pomp be matched by impressive content, by developed ideas, is not after all to violate any contract. If there are ideas in Milton—and there are—they must somehow be worthy of the vehicle in which they are expressed. They must fulfill whatever expectations may justly be formed by an attentive reading of the words of the poem. If a poem is altogether remote from the expression of ideas, or if its dominating mood is incantatory, we may not wish to demand that it be anything but what it is. Leavis is perfectly willing to make such discriminations. He carefully exempts *Comus* from the strictures he directs at *Paradise Lost*, not on the grounds that it is incantatory— like *Lycidas*—but on the grounds that we find there "a kind of action in the verse" that is quite alien to Milton's "Grand Style." Everywhere the critic must attempt to

8. See Davie's *Articulate Energy* (Boston: Routledge & Kegan Paul, 1955), p. 102.

look at the work as it really is, as it really invites us to respond to it.

But we are engaged still on the issue of Milton's failure to deliver a kind of "sustained analytic and discursive thinking" which, in other contexts, Leavis has not thought to require of poets. Among the suggestive notions to be found in the Milton essays is the view that Milton doesn't provide what the reader has a right to expect from his major poems. This is not a problem limited to Milton in Leavis's reading of the English tradition. Wherever we turn there is an insistence upon *adequacy*, which is the expression of significant experience warranted by the text itself and the transaction it invites. *Paradise Lost* promises more than music. It cannot be said to satisfy the expectations it generates by attaching us to words in the way that the poet is himself attached to them—in part for their own sake. The poem promises more various attachments. Neither can it attach us to simple attitudes. In Leavis's terms, Milton is, "for the purposes of his undertaking, disastrously single-minded and simple-minded. He reveals everywhere a dominating sense of righteousness and a complete incapacity to question or explore its significance and conditions. This defect of intelligence is a defect of imagination." The reader will, hopefully, want to overlook the categorical and hyperbolic temper of the passage and attend to its relevant conceptual thrust. Leavis objects to Milton's work, it would seem, because in promising to do a great deal, it reduces a vastly complex subject to more or less unitary dimensions. That the poem is architecturally grand, that it is an edifice with many splendid rooms and views, no one will dispute. But that these elements may be said to correspond to genuine intricacies of the matter at issue, Leavis will have us deny. Again, the reader's disposition here must be uncertain. It is hard enough to feel ungrateful in one's relation with a work so vastly impressive and intermittently absorbing as *Paradise Lost*. It is doubly difficult to yield to Leavis's sometimes shrill declamations on the poem when these are unaccompanied by detailed textual analysis of an appropriate sort.

But there is more to say of Leavis's critique, and what we say may well take us in the direction of those alternate text references we've had a mind to consult. If Milton may be said to be magniloquent, he may with equal damage be said to have succumbed to an unexamined sense of righteousness: this, at least, Leavis would have us believe. But why should a righteous temper be thought inimical to the purposes of a poem like *Paradise Lost*? This is a crucial question that is nowhere directly addressed by the critic. Would Leavis challenge a poet's disposition to ironic understatement in the same way? I think not, though I am not at all sure I can determine a reason. Perhaps there is something in a righteous habit of mind that, if it is to be persuasively enacted in a dramatic or epic poem, simply requires that it think a little skeptically about itself. One hesitates to suggest that Leavis is uncomfortable with Milton's righteousness because it goes against the grain of his own temper, or because it violates implicit attitudes toward creation that have been for some time firmly established in our culture. Surely Leavis would himself dispute such notions. But we have a stated objection to make sense of, and very little to go on in the way of, extended expository analysis. If Leavis objects to Milton's righteousness, we have to know why this particular attitude should seem objectionable when others that are equally unexamined do not.

While righteousness has never in itself seemed an especially appealing attitude to Leavis—to judge only from his published writings—he has never seemed uncomfortable about piety or religious aspiration. His feeling for Eliot's work, especially for "Ash Wednesday" and "Four Quartets," would seem to prove the point. In praising Pope he can go so far as to recommend certain poems even to readers with unregenerate romantic standards: at his best, says Leavis, "his contemplation is religious in its seriousness."[9] Perhaps, then, the thrust of Leavis's objection to Milton has more to do with the fact that his righteousness, so-called, is unexamined, that the poet has not thought to account for it. In speaking of Milton's incapacity to explore the "conditions" of his righteousness, Leavis may be working within the tried limits of his own usual requirements. A righteous habit of mind is required to account for itself because it is notoriously subject to empty assertion and oracular presentment. Ironic understatement may be cheaply won, no doubt, but it is nowhere likely to sweep up a reader and numb the collaborative intelligence in the way that righteous declamation may. Why doesn't Leavis say as much in the essay on Milton? Probably because there are some things he wants to take for granted and cannot bring himself to say everything each time he wants to say one thing. There are other reasons, of course, that have to do with Leavis's belief in a community of educated persons and shared assumptions that, if not dependable in the way he'd like to believe, can be counted on in the imposing of basic requirements at least. But this is a subject we'll look into at another point.

For the moment, let us accept that, for Leavis, righteousness in a poem like Milton's has to account for itself because, when it does not, it asks the reader to yield too easily to its attitudes and messages. From this, it is but a short step to the recognition that Leavis in effect asks nothing more of Milton's poem than he would of any other. That is to say, the understanding of the way a poem

9. See the essay on Pope in *Revaluation*.

16

works, of the process of thought it expresses, is entirely of a piece with the criticism he has written on very different figures. Consider his work on the metaphysical poets. The stress is on what Leavis calls the "irresistible rightness" of Donne, the "representative" strength of Carew, the "tough reasonableness of Marvell's lyric grace," his "wide range of varied and maturely valued interests."[10] At their best, Leavis is assiduous to argue, "it is not any eccentric or defiant audacity that makes the effect here so immediate." This is an important departure from Dr. Johnson and from many subsequent students of metaphysical extravagance. The poetry of wit may feature an intellectual dimension that is rather different from what we expect in Wordsworth or in Keats, but we do not on that account conclude it is *essentially* distinct from other kinds of mature writing. Milton's poem, in failing to treat the "conditions" of its dominating attitudes, fails to operate in terms required of any successful poem. It is not the "prose attitude of mind" that Leavis wants to find in Milton, any more than he would demand of Donne the kind of "order and connectedness" he values in Pope. Neither does he object to unusual effects or audacious tropes—such as we find in Hopkins—so long as the eccentricity is not cultivated for its own sake, or for the sake of the "cheap" effects it may generate. Milton is judged by an implicit standard according to which his more ambitious work fails by failing to think through its materials in the necessary ways.

The poem as thought: this is a notion that no one has done more to define and promote than Leavis. It is vital to his understanding of literature and of the role of literary creation in culture. His discussion of metaphysical verse is so interesting because it indicates, again and again, how central to our concern for poetry as poetry is

10. See "The Line of Wit" in *Revaluation*, pp. 11, 15, 26, 30.

17

a proper appreciation of what the metaphysicals really do, how they think through their materials. It is not the effects produced that are of paramount interest to Leavis, though the effects will perhaps weigh most heavily in our initial response to the poems themselves. As always, Leavis values something else, which is the *control* of ingenuities and effects by "a total imaginative or emotional purpose." This is a dimension that he elaborates with telling impact in the study of " 'Thought' and Emotional Quality."[11] The focus isn't Milton, but the moving focus on poets like Shelley, Tennyson, and Donne is legitimately susceptible to any sort of extension we might wish to make. Thought is the pivot of Leavis's unfolding argument: where there is emotional strength in a poem, there will be a series of checks provided by thought. To express an attitude in a convincing way is to subject it to some measure of "disinterested valuation." This is a function of thought, the absence of which Leavis persuasively indicts in analyses of well-known anthology pieces by Tennyson and Shelley, among others. But it is in the discussion of thought as it operates properly that Leavis does his most important work.

Metaphysical poets are not always deeply moved by the experience of which they write. When they are so moved, Leavis argues, "we have poetry of very exceptional emotional strength." He adduces as "proof" Donne's "Nocturnall," though he might with equal force have selected other items. "The part of 'Thought' in this strength," he goes on to say, "deserves more consideration than it usually gets under the head of 'Metaphysical wit': there is more to it than subtle ratiocination—the surprising play of analogy. The activity of the thinking mind, the energy of intelligence involved in the meta-

11. Part I of a long five-part work entitled "Judgment and Analysis." It appears in *The Living Principle*.

physical habit means that, when the poet has urgent personal experience to deal with, it is attended to and contemplated—which in turn means some kind of separation, or distinction, between experiencer and experience." One cannot but think here of Eliot's famous essay on "The Metaphysical Poets" (1921),[12] for Leavis's emphasis is quite the contrary of Eliot's, despite their shared admiration for Donne and his confreres. Eliot stresses the fact that "a thought for Donne was an experience; it modified his sensibility"; later poets, like Tennyson and Browning, who have been afflicted by a *dissociation* of sensibility, "do not feel their thought as immediately as the odour of a rose." For Eliot, then, primary concern is for the immediacy with which a thought is felt; for Leavis, what matters is that thought of an appropriate sort take place at all. Eliot sees the thinking and feeling faculties as tending toward a disastrous separation in the years following the seventeenth century. Leavis is not persuaded by the historical terms of the argument and is concerned only that we may fail to register what invariably occurs when a poem succeeds—in the seventeenth, eighteenth, or nineteenth centuries. Where Eliot worries over separation, Leavis insists upon the necessary "separation, or distinction, between experiencer and experience" as a *condition* of thought. I should say that Leavis's is the more subtle and cogent argument.

But what does it mean to say that the poem, as a mode of thought, must enforce a separation between the experiencer and his experience? To understand the point is to see that it refers, not alone to the poet who feels and recollects and records, but to the reader who attends and registers and responds with his own recreative skills. The separation of which Leavis speaks is made possible by the

12. Included in the standard edition of Eliot's *Selected Essays* (New York: Harcourt Brace & Co., 1950).

activity of analysis. This is an activity that has for so long been relegated to secondary status in considerations of artistic process that we should not find it difficult to appreciate the radical unfamiliarity of Leavis's approach. That analysis may be said to have played a part in the composing of metaphysical verse most commentators have been willing to concede. That it is, quintessentially, a creative faculty few even now would accept. So entrenched is the bias against analysis as a secondary, critical faculty—in the English-speaking countries especially —that Leavis may justly be said to argue entirely against the grain in his attempt to make of poetry a mode of *thought*. For thought is, as Leavis has it, inevitably involved in analysis, and analysis enforces distinctions and separations of a kind that passionately intuitive creator–spirits are not often likely to approve. Why do we analyze when we think? Because we wish to connect one thought to another and to judge the validity of thoughts and feelings by appropriate standards. But this is not all. We analyze when we think because there is no help for it. To think is to ask real questions and to set up resistances to easy answers that inevitably clamor to be taken in. Analysis retards the readiness with which we incline to yield to simple formulations, plangent sentiments, and easy answers. It is not an ornament to thought but a constitutive element without which thought must be something else.

No doubt Leavis means more in his use of the term *analysis*, as in his understanding of judgment, than we have yet precisely articulated. In the passage on the metaphysicals we have been considering, he goes on as follows: "to analyze your experience you must, while keeping it alive and immediately present as experience, treat it in some sense as an object. That is, an essential part of the strength of good Metaphysical poetry turns out to be

20

of the same order as the strength of all the most satisfying poetry." This strength is nothing less than the "essential presence of 'thought'. . . . It can be said in favour of the Metaphysical habit that it favours such a presence."[13] Analysis, then, as an indivisible function of thought, depends upon an objectification of experience. The poet works to keep the raw experience alive and immediate while treating it as something apart from him, something not by nature his. The reader of the poem knows it as something given, something manifestly present and available, which yet forbids that he take automatic possession. As the poet may not entirely close the gap between his experience and himself, the reader may not pretend to take in the primary fact of *his* immediate experience—the poem—as if a simple act of interpretative penetration or sympathetic vibration entitled him to possess it unequivocally. Implicit in Leavis's account of analysis is an ethics of literary creation and re-creation. Though anyone may loosely be said to think, to *have* a thought in Leavis's sense is to earn a title that will never be granted upon simple request. The objectification of experience is an enterprise requiring discipline and control. That these are to be regarded as virtues, no student of Leavis may doubt.

Milton was criticized, we recall, for a failure to account for a dominating attitude; also, for an incapacity to do "sustained analytic and discursive thinking"—in his poems, at least. The absence of these components has everything to do with what Leavis means when he speaks of the objectification of experience. For Milton's failure is, in Leavis's view, no simple failure to do this thing or that, any one of which may be incidental to the realization of a particular literary enterprise. It is a failure of thought, and in a poet, this is unavoidably a failure of

13. See " 'Thought' and Emotional Quality" in *The Living Principle*.

imagination. Can a great poet be said to suffer from a general failure of imagination? The question needs to be put, though no one seems finally to have come up with a suitable answer. Milton's great gifts—Leavis never doubts he had them—were enough to produce great music, scattered passages of moving rhetoric. In *Comus* he created a fully living poem. If he never came to use his gifts as he might have, a properly responsive reading will discover why. "In the end we find ourselves protesting," Leavis writes, and goes on to search out the origins and validity of this protest. In Milton, the inability to objectify experience is part of an infatuation with words, with the power and musical variety of his own finely tuned instrument. His addiction to "impressive pomp and volume" is not a failure of character—this much Leavis grants. It is the mark of a spirit that has succumbed to its own experience. Milton identifies with the experience of righteous feeling that he wishes to evoke and to exalt. His feeling for words is a feeling for the swelling emotion they may be observed to release in him and in others. Had he "a capacity for feeling *through* words" he would stand a little apart from them, considering the range of possible meanings and suggestions they can be made to exhibit. He would relate to the words as flexible instrumentalities only partially and temporarily in his keeping. To have objectified his experience would have meant, for Milton, to have resisted the mastery of materials conferred by his own genius and eagerly developed skills. Resistance of that kind is a distinction of intelligence because it ensures that the mastery and the effects it produces will serve the ends truly demanded by the project at hand.

It may be that the argument does not fully persuade where Milton is concerned. Though the studies of Milton are among the most audacious things that Leavis ever wrote—and he had the example of Eliot to provide some support—it isn't clear that the general estimate of Milton in the academy has been permanently affected.[14] It may be that literary academics have too great a stake in Milton to be favorably moved by any attack, but I prefer to believe that, had Leavis pursued the argument in greater detail, he might have won the day. No one will imagine that the studies on Milton may be easily dismissed. For our purposes, they indicate how often it is necessary, in reading Leavis, to provide illumination for one study by bringing in relevant material from another. This should not be alarming for students of imaginative literature. Everyone knows how difficult it is to understand what Yeats was working toward in "Adam's Curse" without knowing something about his earlier work in the nineties. We are perfectly willing to explain or to flesh out an attitude of James in *What Maisie Knew* by looking at character prototypes in an earlier novel like *The Portrait of a Lady*. Students of a body of criticism should have comparable procedural advantages.

If the Milton studies don't fully persuade, they do raise in an explicit way several of the major issues that the student of Leavis will want to consider. We have, in our discussion, already brought into focus key terms like *analysis*, *objectification*, *thought*, and *adequacy*. Though none of these is definitively elaborated in the Milton studies—we had to go outside our two primary texts to come up with them—all are essential to a grasp of the main argument. We've resisted focused elaboration of terms like *judgment* and *the living principle* because they cannot be gotten at without further exposition of Leavis's criticism. Several of the major issues are before us. With

14. Eliot's first Milton essay had a substantial impact, of course, but it may hardly be said to have permanently altered Milton's stature.

Milton, the key terms were instrumental to a severe judgment that is nowhere contemptuous or routinely dismissive. Applied to other figures, the terms are likely to open up other issues no less important.

Leavis has made notoriously poor—that is, indefensible—judgments about a number of writers who deserve more respectful criticism. Virginia Woolf is one of these; Scott Fitzgerald is another. The dismissal of Joyce as a creative dead end and a waste of time hasn't affected critical estimates in the slightest, but it has generated serious misgiving about the discriminative powers of a consistently judicial criticism. Joyce is too large to tackle here, and Leavis has not had enough to say about the major work to make the enquiry valuable. The dismissals of Woolf and Fitzgerald are also too casual and unsustained to require attention. The one contemporary figure who has consistently been given a hard time by Leavis, while enjoying great critical esteem, is W. H. Auden. A genuinely "intellectual" poet with a fine ear and considerable range, he seems a suitable case on which to test some of the ideas earlier singled out. Though Leavis has not thought to devote a full-length study to Auden—a deplorable omission, I should say—he has thought about him almost to the point of obsession. This much we conclude by registering the frequency and the virulence of references to Auden and his colleagues—Stephen Spender, especially—in Leavis's work. The student of Leavis who has collected the many brief reviews and references to Auden will know almost how to write for Leavis the extensive essay on the poet he never wrote.

Auden could never be accused of being uninterested in ideas or incapable of sustained discursive thinking. That is why he makes so useful a test case, after our investigation of Milton. In many ways Auden ought to appeal to Leavis. He wrote a great deal, had much to say about all sorts of experience, and seemed very much in touch both with the advanced thought and the more elusive currents of feeling of his time. What is more, he managed to bring his interests, in all their sometimes complex particularity, into the verse without undue simplification. If he had a taste for abstraction that threatened occasionally to get out of hand, he managed most often to express his thoughts in the common language of his day, to write in the accents of a spoken language. Attracted to his own special tropes and "ingrown idiosyncrasy"[15]—one thinks of all the capitalized and personified abstractions around which entire poems are sometimes built—he yet seemed aware of his own dubious predilections and had a capacity to think against the grain of the verse when the occasion seemed appropriate. Milton may have failed to sustain analysis, to objectify experience, but Auden may be said to have specialized in using poetry to think discursively and precisely about his experience. At its best, the poetry is not applied to the exposition and resolution of ideas; it gives the impression of generating ideas out of its engagement with several recurrent impressions and formulated perceptions. The critic who, like Leavis, values the writer's sense of process and of poised encounter with his own delicate awareness might have been expected to find in Auden *his* poet.

Auden was, from the first, a presence in the English literary scene. He had a number of gifted and versatile associates, and his own gifts were such as to indicate at once that he might do extraordinary things. Leavis and his colleagues at *Scrutiny* took notice of the poet as one might of a precocious young fellow who has everything going for him but who has not the sense to ask one's advice on exactly how and where to proceed. Though the

15. Leavis says as much of Hopkins in *New Bearings in English Poetry*.

criticism is directed at the poetry, there is a quality of personal animus everywhere apparent, especially in Leavis's observations. One feels, unmistakably, the critic's intuitive distaste for a young man with loyal and generous friends to whom he is so attentive as to include them—by name or by implication—in his verse. In a 1936 review of Auden, Leavis detects, "not only a complete absence of exposure to criticism, but also a confident awareness of an encouraging audience."[16] In a later (1951) piece, on the English literary scene, Leavis holds it against Auden that he should have inspired "undergraduate" effusions from youthful friends like Spender; worse, the quality of response typically evoked by the poet is no better in the review columns printed by *The Times Literary Supplement*.[17] Though he nowhere says it outright, Leavis suggests that Auden would have been better off had he never been encouraged by people who saw in him the promise of major achievement. Had he been just a little less precocious, had he written less polished and striking shorter poems in his youth, Auden might have "grown up" in a way that would have permitted him to do justice to his real gifts. No one would have asked him to produce major poems before his thirtieth birthday, and he would not have felt compelled to enlarge the range of experience treated in his work beyond anything he might have been said to know or to feel. The criticism opened up by Leavis himself is echoed in other pieces produced by a variety of *Scrutiny* contributors during the thirties and forties. Thus, R. G. Lienhardt, in a 1945 re-

16. See "Mr. Auden's Talent," reprinted in *A Selection from Scrutiny* (Cambridge, Eng.: Cambridge University Press, 1968), 1:110–14.

17. See "Mr. Pryce-Jones, The British Council and British Culture," reprinted in *A Selection from Scrutiny*, 1: esp. pp. 188–89.

view of Auden's *For the Time Being*, speaks of the poet's "morbidity and disillusion" as "in fact nothing more than a fashionable accretion, perhaps unconscious and unavoidable." The cause? He has been "impervious to criticism from outside the group which formed his ideal public, and which existed on a basis of mutual admiration which a more independent poet would have found an embarrassment."[18]

One has no hesitation in adducing Lienhardt and Robin Mayhead, another *Scrutiny* contributor, as witness to the thrust of Leavis's criticism. *Scrutiny* was a collaborative enterprise, and though Leavis surely did not approve of everything that appeared in its pages, the Auden criticism he collected and published is entirely of a piece. If Leavis did not choose to write more on Auden, the reason may well have been that his colleagues carried the attack so well. At any rate, the disapproval of Auden on "personal" and "political" grounds, consistently developed in the various *Scrutiny* pieces, may hardly be said to be incidental to the evolution of his work as a poet. Nor is it possible to speak of the disapproval as at any point "merely" personal or crudely political. One may not *like* a criticism that incorporates references to a poet's friends and all-too-approving public, but that is something different from disputing the validity of the main argument. Auden exhibited a persistent tendency "to indulge in verbal virtuosity for its own sake," to "escape from the responsibility of integrating language and experience"; more important, though there are ideas and "interests," there is over all a "lack of urgency, lack of conviction, lack of real interest"; the assumed postures are too often "adolescent," promising "no maturity of

18. See R. G. Lienhardt, "Auden's Inverted Development," reprinted in *A Selection from Scrutiny*, 1:115–19.

outlook."[19] This is the dominant thrust of the Leavisian critique of Auden, here expressed by a trusted colleague. To understand the verse, and what it invites us to feel, is to address such issues.

The reader will see at once that, while Auden has very little in common with Milton (though both may be said to have had substantial linguistic and technical endowments), it is possible to speak of their deficiencies in comparable terms. But so different is the feel of their verse, the texture of the language and tone of the articulating voice, that it would be misleading really to speak of one in the context of the other. In discussing Auden's poise and sense of audience, it may be appropriate to speak of someone like Pope, but there too the discriminations required are considerable. For the moment, it is more appropriate to place in focus the several counters on which Leavis particularly depends for his critique of Auden. Neither *thought* nor *analysis* figures prominently in the description of the poet's deficiencies. The word *adequacy*, suggesting the capacity of the work to deliver what it promises, is more useful, though not precisely right either. Auden may be said, in Leavis's terms, to *obectify his experience*, but in this case the achievement seems not to merit critical approval.

What needs, then, to be said? Leavis writes, in an unusually brief review of *Another Time* (1940): "That poised knowledgeableness, that impressive command of the modern scene, points to the conditions in which his promise has lost itself."[20] The imputation of "knowledgeableness" is central to our concern with Auden, as

19. Robin Mayhead, "The Latest Auden" (1952), reprinted in *A Selection from Scrutiny*, 1:120–25.
20. See "Auden's Talent," reprinted in *A Selection from Scrutiny*, 1:114.

it is seen to be in every critique of the poet published in *Scrutiny*. The word suggests, does it not, that it is possible to know too much about the wrong things. Is this what Leavis means to say? But if he wants Auden to know less about European history, or about Freudian theory, he ought surely to say so. That he does not should indicate that he objects, not to what Auden knows, or *that* he knows, but to what his knowing makes of him *in his verse*. To speak of "poised knowledgeableness" is to point to a capacity to know without being ruffled, for better or for worse, by what one has learned. To be knowledgeable is to know, shall we say, a variety of things, some or most of which may not be worth knowing. To remain poised, at all costs, is to know some things in what most of us would take to be an inauthentic way. If Auden exhibits, everywhere, a poised knowledgeableness, there will be something false or shallow in his relation to his experience. That is Leavis's contention.

That Auden's "virtues," to which Leavis so objects, are worlds apart from the virtues exhibited by many other poets of whom the critic approves, can tell us nothing of importance. Leavis takes frank delight in the poise exhibited by Pope and has nothing but admiration for the range of knowledge and interest we find in Marvell. These admirations do not compromise the affection he feels for a very different poet, like Hopkins. His objection to Auden is *particular*, however founded on standards we can show to be extensible to other contexts. Auden's tone of command, his poise and flexibility, are negative virtues for several reasons: 1) There is "an embarrassing uncertainty" about what it is that requires to be so controlled; 2) Auden has a "tendency to make a virtue" of his inclinations, that is, to flatter himself that they are "becoming"; 3) The command is managed through the achievement of small ironies that are in large measure either "self-defen-sive" or "self-indulgent"; 4) Auden's command, which should permit him to work toward the solving of prob-lems, in fact "conceals a failure to grapple with them"; 5) Instead of flexibly accommodating a range of experi-ences in order to organize them strictly and inevitably, even Auden's "most serious work exhibits a shameless opportunism in the passage from phrase to phrase and from item to item."[21]

The attack on Auden, confident and consistent, does not rely upon detailed quotation from the verse. Leavis here seems to feel that his "essential judgments" will be accepted "by reason of their manifest irresistibleness"—a standard upon which first-rate criticism may be said to depend.[22] The fundamental contention, that Auden lacks conviction and is therefore false or shallow, is more diffi-cult to prove by selective quotation than the other charges. This in itself does not disqualify the broad charge, but it does demand that it be set aside pending fuller examina-tion of the relevant verse. In this case, the relevant verse cannot be said to consist of everything the poet published. If Leavis's charges are persuasive, they must be per-suasive in respect to the best things Auden wrote. Our selection of telling passages in Auden, then, must be drawn from the verse the poet himself wished to preserve; verse, moreover, that "friendly" critics have generally approved. Leavis's judgments may not be irresistible, but they do have a splendid compactness and force that ought to enable verification without involving us in unnecessary ambiguity or special pleading. Since the critic has himself relied in most instances on verification by quotation and

21. All quotations here from Leavis's reviews of Auden re-printed in *A Selection from Scrutiny*, 1:110–14.
22. See " 'English,' Unrest and Continuity" in *Nor Shall My Sword*, p. 112.

example, we can do no less where a poet of Auden's current stature is concerned.[23]

Point 1—uncertainty:

> Lay your sleeping head, my love,
> Human on my faithless arm;
> Time and fevers burn away
> Individual beauty from
> Thoughtful children, and the grave
> Proves the child ephemeral:
> But in my arms till break of day
> Let the living creature lie,
> Mortal, guilty, but to me
> The entirely beautiful.
>
> (from "Lullaby")[24]

If I am not mistaken, the poem "Lullaby" has for long been a favorite of Auden's admirers. It has the advantage of representativeness: no literary person reading the poem would fail at once to recognize it as a sample of Auden's special voice. It is perhaps more unequivocally tender and urgent than most of Auden's better poems, but these qualities do not substantially compromise the point of the control on which Auden typically relies. Where is the uncertainty Leavis so reproves? Consider the word "faithless" in the second line. In what sense is the lover faithless? There is nothing in the poem to indicate any specific capacity of betrayal in the speaker. Though he tells us, three stanzas later, that "Beauty, midnight, vision dies," we don't know really that he will betray his current vision of his loved one by taking another lover or denying what he feels. "Faithless" as it is used relates more certainly to

23. Eliot often spoke of felicitous quotation as "the best evidence of taste," and Leavis would seem to have concurred. See Leavis's essay on Arnold in *A Selection from Scrutiny*, 1: esp. p. 260.

24. Opening stanza of "Lullaby" from *Selected Poetry of W. H. Auden*, second edition (Vintage, 1971). All subsequent quotations from Auden are from this edition of poems selected "by the author."

the word "ephemeral" in line six than to any other word in the poem. We are faithless, the speaker suggests, in the sense that we are mortal, subject to change. What is more, he goes on, there is nothing, really, that we can do about the changes that come to pass. If "time and fevers burn away" not merely what we feel, but what we are, how may we suppose ourselves responsible in any enduring way? And yet, the poem implicitly contends, there is a control we are required to maintain. We must put a pleasant face on things. In the space of operations given to us, we must "let the living creature lie," refuse to disturb it in what is necessarily an ignorant contentment. As he utters the words "to me/ The entirely beautiful," does the speaker mean that his loved one seems indeed without flaw as he beholds, or that the equation controlling the poem requires some such utterance to convey the mildly ironic poise with which he grasps, appropriately, our ephemererality?

When Leavis speaks of uncertainty, then, and says that it is "embarrassing," he may mean to indicate that Auden resists giving himself away even in poems whose ostensive burden is that we can do nothing but love unreasonably in the face of what we know. The irony of "the entirely beautiful" qualifies feeling by making it an object of a very special sort of play that is indistinguishable from control. This control is at odds with the speaker's insistence that we are subject creatures who lullaby to one another knowing full well that our attachments are "faithless." In the end, the control seems confused and, yes, in the constant worked-up poise with which it is articulated, embarrassing. For what is it from which the poem wishes to distance us: from the generous and loving sentiment of the poem's presented moment, or from the knowledge of faithless instability at the heart of things? Once, in stanza two, the speaker refers to the "abstract insight" which may disturb us in the business of our "ordinary" lives. Is it unfair to suggest that Auden's poise and control in this poem, as in others, are a function of "abstract insight" itself imprecisely understood and "placed"?

Point 2—making a virtue of uncertainty and other dubious achievements:

> One circumlocution as used as any
> Depends, it seems, upon the joke of rhyme
> For the pure joy; else why should so many
> Poems which make us cry direct us to
> Ourselves at our least apt, least kind, least true,
> Where a blank I loves blankly a blank You?
>> (from "One Circumlocution")

> I should like to become, if possible,
>   a minor Atlantic Goethe,
> with his passion for weather and stones but without his
>   silliness re the Cross: at times a bore, but,
> while knowing Speech can at best, a shadow echoing
>   the silent light, bear witness
> to the Truth it is not, he wished it were, as the Francophile
>   gaggle of pure songsters
> are too vain to. We're no musicians: to stink of Poetry
>   is unbecoming, and never
> to be dull shows a lack of taste. Even a limerick
>   ought to be something a man of
> honor, awaiting death from cancer or a firing squad,
>   could read without contempt: (at
> *that* frontier I wouldn't dare speak to anyone
>   in either a prophet's bellow
> or a diplomat's whisper.)
>> (from "The Cave of Making")

Two passages from two very different poems. In the first, the entire poem not much more than a pointed jest, the poet reduces his craft to a dubious sort of mastery. Is it plausible to wonder why poems assume the shapes in which we come to know them? There is an explanation, frequently sufficient: "the joke of rhyme/ For the pure joy;" and, lest we imagine that "rhyme" refers exclusively

33

to the repetition of sound, the poet so concludes his poem that the word takes on much greater resonance. What do poems do? They work out their materials. According to what principle? That one thing ought deftly to follow another. What do you do if you don't like what you come up with, which you know to be—in the language of the second stanza—a "compromise"? Bear in mind that there are other versions, other selves to which we might just as well have been directed. All will be well.

"One Circumlocution" gives us an Auden with whom we are all too familiar.[25] If he tends to make a virtue of uncertainty, he does so here with a sort of silly cleverness that trivializes everything it touches. He wants, after all, both to suggest that he is endlessly clever where artifactual devices are concerned and that he knows as well what things are true. Nowhere, of course, does he actually commit himself to telling us the truth, to calling things by the rightful names that confer significance. To do so might compromise his alternative commitment to his own cunning devices and the evasions they enable. To look ahead to point three, the ironies here are "self-defensive and self-indulgent." They protect Auden from having to consider what, in fact, his propositions amount to. They permit him to play with words—stanzas one and three give us, respectively, "The out-there-when we are already in" and "The once-for-all that is not seen nor said"— without having to own up or pursue them to anything concrete that would constitute their realization.

Our second passage, from a longer, more discursive poem Auden describes toward the close as an "egocentric monologue," does no better to satisfy the Leavisian stan-

25. To see how much better this kind of poem can be done, look into some of Howard Nemerov's gnomic utterances. A "Son of Auden," Nemerov has done things ever so much better than the older poet.

dard. Juggling its learned references deftly in an attempt to elegize Auden's old friend, Louis MacNeice, it leaves us with the feeling that we've been invited to listen in on some amiable chitchat—monologous, of course, but with some achieved sense of friendly give and take. Of what does Auden here attempt to make a virtue? First, of not knowing who is to be the focus of the poem; or better yet, of not caring really whether or not it has a center. Comfortable relations, after all, in the perspective of this poem, will be founded on the good sense that they are one in the same with refusing to insist strenuously upon anything. This is an attitude which, whatever we may think of it, is not in itself open to strictly aesthetic criticism. That is to say, the objection we may raise to the attitude, insofar as it is a legitimate objection, will have to dwell upon the function of the attitude in the poem. This, Leavis has persistently reminded us, is the least we can do.[26]

In "The Cave of Making," the attitude described is correlative to a sense of friendship the poet wishes to celebrate. What is this friendship? It is a fellowship in poetry, in letters, a fellowship whose ethic is none other than good taste, minor ambition, and genial forbearance. If there is an aesthetic objection to the attitudes as they are elaborated, it is that they are obvious and intolerably self-regarding; that they are easy to assume, and cost nothing to abandon. (What trouble would it be for an Auden to state that, in the end, he'd want to speak to ultimate issues in a more strenuous, even a more pretentious

26. One of Leavis's better critics, Vincent Buckley, has argued rather cogently that he sometimes judges a work "too highly because he has a temperamental affinity with the predominating attitude," especially when, as in the case of Hardy, the attitude is "a sort of stoicism in a minor key." But, for the most part, the critic has been as good as his word in his treatment of writers. See Buckley's *Poetry and Morality* (London: Chatto & Windus, 1959), pp. 171–72.

or "prophetic" way? Even someone used to speaking in a minor key may think to raise the pitch just a bit as he anticipates the final clap. That Auden resists any such "display," here as elsewhere, only suggests how limiting his assumed poise has been.) The attitudes so celebrated would seem, in themselves, to have nothing in them that would warrant their being expressed as virtues. No one would think to call them values, or to propose them as standards to which human beings might aspire. They are objectionable in the degree to which the poet makes of them a general good. Had he been content to keep clear what it was he felt, to distinguish it from what others might justly be expected to experience or desire, Auden would have done better by his friendship.

But in what sense may this unwarranted attribution of general value be said to consort with the failure to assign the poem a center? Auden makes a virtue of necessity and calls it freedom.[27] This is just the sort of intellectual dishonesty Leavis has noted all through Auden's career. The poet has a number of predilections to which he is strongly attached. Leavis calls them "private neuroses and memories," and the designation seems fair enough. Instead of using the poem to evoke them in their particularity, thereby to free himself of what may be unwanted or, at least, unwarrantable, he plays with them in what Leavis terms "an essentially immature way." If the poem had a center, it might be forced to work out its thoughts as one does in an accounting. By trying on this, then that, then another thought, by spreading itself whimsically, the poem attributes value without enacting it. It is in the nature of a successful poem not to be able to

27. A point made in detail by Randall Jarrell, among others. See the Auden essays in Jarrell's *The Third Book of Criticism* (New York: Farrar, Straus & Giroux, Inc., 1969).

affect insouciance with anything approaching perfect adequacy. Always there must be, even in such a poem, an underlying pressure to get at something with a precision previously missed. By treating lightly what isn't in general to be taken lightly, and failing to indicate or to generate the attitude that ought properly to be taken, Auden falsifies his materials. What is "a man of honor"? What can it mean to "bear witness to the Truth"? In the perspective of Auden's poem, such things do not clamor to be fixed or pondered. The poet has made a virtue of being too sensible to be overly worried about anything, including the very words to which, in the very nature of his medium, he invariably resorts.

Points 3 and 4—irony as self-defense and self-indulgence; failing to grapple with problems:

> I, too, am reproached, for what
> And how much you know. Not to lose time, not to get caught,
> Not to be left behind, not, please! to resemble
> The beasts who repeat themselves, or a thing like water
> Or stone whose conduct can be predicted, these
> Are our Common Prayer, whose greatest comfort is music
> Which can be made anywhere, is invisible,
> And does not smell. In so far as we have to look forward
> To death as a fact, no doubt we are right: but if
> Sins can be forgiven, if bodies rise from the dead,
> These modifications of matter into
> Innocent athletes and gesticulating fountains,
> Made solely for pleasure, make a further point:
> The blessed will not care what angle they are regarded from,
> Having nothing to hide. Dear, I know nothing of
> Either, but when I try to imagine a faultless love
> Or the life to come, what I hear is the murmur
> Of underground streams, what I see is a limestone landscape.
> (from "In Praise of Limestone")

"In Praise of Limestone" may not be Auden's most popular poem, but it is surely one of his most ambitious and complex works. Though it lacks the fine precision and music of "The Shield of Achilles" or the stately elegiac brilliance of "In Memory of Sigmund Freud," it is an impressive combination of audacious contrivance and careful psychological analysis. We have seen that Auden's is often not "the irony of a mature mind," as Leavis says. In one poem after another we feel ourselves in the presence of a thought that is anxious not to know what it is about, while pretending to a control that is comprehensive and unruffled. In "Limestone," though, Leavis's argument confronts a difficult test. The postures remain, the attitudes more or less what we've observed. The irony is pervasive, intermittently obvious with the solemnity of the overbrilliant "adolescent" Leavis has detected—witness the opening: "If it form the one landscape that we the inconstant ones / Are consistently homesick for, this is chiefly / Because it dissolves in water." But the irony even there can hardly be said to be merely adolescent. It has a point to make, knows itself to be clever, and keeps the two dimensions well in hand, each in its proper place. The point is undercut ever so mildly by the attendant irony built into the unstable idiom developed in the sentence. But the point is no less clear or determinative of what is to follow, for all that it has been *placed* by the opening irony in the texture of the speaking voice. For Auden's point is precisely that, given what we have made of ourselves in the various periods of Western history, we have nothing to look to *but* the attitudes associated with limestone. There is nothing dishonest or defensive about this. The irony conceals nothing: Auden defines with tremendous tact and precision what the irony is good for and what general understanding it expresses. At no moment does he pretend to be aloof from the general attitudes surveyed. Where there is difference, it is revealed, not simply attributed, as a matter either of personal preference or of cultural disposition. Everything is accorded its due. The imagination that works over everything with a terrific synthesizing compactness yet manages its little grace notes. No irony is wasted or cheaply bought, no target hit without some accompanying reminder of how it got to be targeted.

Why should Auden have managed in the "Limestone" poem what he could not manage elsewhere?[28] It may be that, as Leavis has argued, more scrupulous early criticism might have helped. But it is in the nature of poets not to be able to know what exactly makes for their greatest successes. If they knew, the better poets would write fewer bad poems than they write. Consider "Limestone," how easily it might squander its advantages: how, for example, its "Not to lose time, not to get caught, / Not to be left behind, not, please! to resemble / The beasts . . . " might be made to display the poet's presumptive superiority; or, how the images of "Innocent athletes and gesticulating fountains" might be made into calculated personifying counters required to flesh out a vision that was fundamentally conceptual and abstract. Here, in just the way that Leavis has so often demanded, the medium "creates what it conveys"; what is presented is "not thought of, but possessed imaginatively in its concreteness."[29] The poem succeeds so well because the speaker's attraction to a limestone landscape and all it may be said to evoke and to recommend is ever so much more palpable than a predictably coy statement of pref-

28. It wasn't for lack of trying that Auden failed generally to reproduce his success. In fact, he wrote a great many poems that, in substance, resemble "Limestone," including "The Horatians" and "Lakes." Without the controlling limestone metaphor, these poems become slight, inadequate statements of personal predilection rather than creative examinations of a tempting emotional terrain.

29. See Leavis on the powers of the enacting medium in "Tragedy and the 'Medium'" in *The Common Pursuit*, esp. pp. 123–24.

erence for a certain kind of life. Where elsewhere Auden seems bent on telling us what he likes and inviting us to admire him for being so clever, in "Limestone" he allows the medium—dominated by the figure of limestone—to discover what it is we need to know to arrive at a judgment. By allowing us to take possession of the landscape, he ensures that we will not be too quick to dismiss it as the product of a shallow or superficial disposition. In a sense, Auden's vision of possibility is shallow, and he knows it. He wants the things that do not cost so very much in painful effort. His attraction to Freud is an attraction to the prospect of a civilized experience that is not founded upon the domination of instinct by guilt. We do not feel compelled, in reading "Limestone," to decide for or against the disposition expressed. We judge only the adequacy of the realization to the conceptual project. The judgment is, as we may say, positive, because we feel that we have come into close imaginative relation with something that is worth knowing.

The irony? It is so obviously *not* defensive that it may unequivocally be said to *illuminate* the petty deceptions and expediencies to which the speaker is himself committed. To be attracted to a music that "does not smell" is, after all, to be placed in a curiously exact and penetrating way. As to self-indulgence, the reader who is suspicious of Auden on the basis of previous experience is well advised to consider whether any detail in the poem resists the general purposes Auden assigns. The irony works because it is an expression of the speaker's close involvement in the limestone landscape he evokes. If the irony promotes a certain detachment, it is not a detachment that permits the speaker to evade implication in or responsibility for what is placed. Leavis has taught us how to make the essential discriminations in such a matter. Irony, he has warned, like other elaborated attitudes in a literary work, may represent nothing more than an opportunity seized. As a poet may be "Seeking a license for an emotional debauch," he may alternatively conceive a situation "in order to have the satisfaction of a disciplined imaginative exercise." What we need to look out for are "marks of the imaginative self-projection that is insufficiently informed by experience": an experience, that is to say, realized within the given poem. Irony, when it is self-indulgent, very much like other modes of "imaginative self-projection," will lack the "convincing concreteness of a presented situation that speaks for itself."[30] When we attend to Auden's irony, is it the situation that we hear through the articulating voice, or the rhetorical preening of the all-knowing *poseur*? I should have to say that the poem resists at every point the imputation of insincerity Leavis has alerted us to expect in Auden.

Nor is there, in "Limestone," the failure to grapple with the problems that Auden regularly elsewhere presents as a readiness to take them on. Every properly critical reader of Auden will know how the poet lets drop, in poem after poem, the impressive signal that he has thought of everything, that no problem has escaped his wary eye. Thus the interpolated forced references to an abstract "History's criminal noise" in one poem ("The Common Life"), or to the historically conditioned ineffectuality of "the private life" as emblematized in the drifting "conversation of the highly trained" in another ("Embassy"). In "Limestone" the problems are grappled with in what Leavis should take to be the proper spirit. There is a sense of what Leavis has described, in another context, as "complete detachment and control" combined

30. Leavis's remarks appear in the "Reality and Sincerity" section of "Judgment and Analysis"; published in *The Living Principle.* See esp. pp. 128–30.

with a realized "pressure of personal experience."[31] Auden wishes to see what he is, to understand precisely the direction of his own fondest thoughts and aspirations. To do this, to get it all down with an indisputable rightness, he must see what are the sources of his disposition— sources not peculiar to him but characteristic of all those who are comparably disposed. The enquiry is not in any academic sense sociological, any more than the analysis of motive and feeling may be said to be strictly psychological. The poem grapples with its issues by allowing us, like Auden, "to 'feel into' or 'become' " the material examined. The least we can say is that Auden succeeds in presenting a *situation* so concretely that it invites us to participate in working through the questions it generates.

Point 5—shameless opportunism in the passage from one item to another:

> Simultaneously, as soundlessly,
>   Spontaneously, suddenly
> As, at the vaunt of the dawn, the kind
>   Gates of the body fly open
> To its world beyond . . .
>   (from "Prime" in the *Horae Canonicae*)

> Come to our well-run desert
> Where anguish arrives by cable
>   And the deadly sins may be bought in tins
> With instructions on the label . . .
>   . . . .
> He is the Way.
> Follow him through the Land of Unlikeness;
> You will see rare beasts, and have unique adventures
>   (from "A Christmas Oratorio")

The problem here, as Leavis would have it, has everything to do with the organizing of material in a work of literature. By organization Leavis understands an operation entirely distinct from simplifying reduction or imitative

31. See the discussion of Pound in *New Bearings in English Poetry*.

logic. The poem at its best—like the novel—disposes its particulars in such a way that together they feel toward "implicit laws" relative to the issues at hand. Where the organization is exclusively verbal or rhetorical, the laws are seen to impose themselves on the material and to allow no intensity of opposition or resistance. Things "go together" for no better reason than that they sound alike or belong "to the general effect" loosely sought. The type of such poetry is Swinburne's.[32] More difficult to diagnose is a poetry that has no doubt about what it wishes to affirm and organizes materials to conduct us to a foreknown conclusion. Such works may make us feel, intermittently, that we are witness to a genuine exploratory–creative procedure, though the general absence of "dialectical suspense and crisis" is likely to produce unease after a while. This could happen even in a poet like Wordsworth, whose didactic urgings won many a "convert" in the nineteenth century.[33] In such verse, the implicit laws are not sought in an appropriately open spirit such as would leave itself susceptible to disappointment and obstruction in its quest. Though the poem may promise rigorous argument and philosophic scruple, it opts in the end for visionary wisdom, which is a very different thing.[34]

To say that, for Leavis, successful organization in poetry is very much what it is in the novel is to indicate at least what he does *not* mean. He does not intend to

32. Leavis disposes of Swinburne nicely, and in short order, in *Revaluation*, pp. 238–40.

33. See Leavis's account in *Revaluation*, pp. 154–85.

34. Donald Davie argues that Leavis is mistaken to locate in Wordsworth an offer of philosophic argument—an offer the verse cannot sustain. What we have, Davie contends, is a poetry of meditation that "is therefore authentic, not a play of misleading forms." It seems to me that, in the passages he chooses to discuss, Leavis has the better of the argument. See Davie's *Articulate Energy*, pp. 110–15.

suggest that organization is in any plain sense a matter of verbal correspondence. The implicit laws to which a work responds are discovered not in "separate local 'meanings' put together more or less felicitously," but in "the totality of the communication."[35] This totality will be realized in one way in prose fiction, in another in Shakespearean verse drama. The principle will be the same, the operating thought entirely similar. The work at hand must in some sense be said to receive the impressions it generates, to receive them because they belong. How do we know they belong? By referring to the dynamics of the work in which they participate. The dynamics of a successful work will be built upon a careful release and working out of "friction and tension—" a communicated "sense of arrest." Where there is no *significant* friction or tension we may have an arena for the exercise of "shameless opportunism."

An Auden poem has a law to which it is responsive. That law may be, in many cases is, external to the dynamics of the poem itself. Where Auden fails, the poem accepts alternations of mood and idea because it can do no other. Helpless before the steady discursive ramble of Auden's delivery, it does what it can to accommodate what is served. It gives no sense of having generated the shifts of figure or focus according to the inevitable laws of its constitution. This might be exemplified in dozens of Auden's best-known poems, but we shall have to be content with the brief excerpts from two. They are selected from the review-essays of Leavis's *Scrutiny* colleagues, Lienhardt and Mayhead, who see in them the kinds of telling deficiency Leavis has himself diagnosed. The passage from "Prime" is discussed by Mayhead as follows:

35. See "Imagery and Movement" in "Judgment and Analysis"; published in *The Living Principle*. See esp. pp. 102–8.

Here, I think it will be agreed, there is a sense of strain, a sense that the poet is trying artificially to inject life into verse that resolutely refuses to leave the ground. For what can the first two lines be said to have achieved? Do the four adverbs, words with a rich potential of associations, signify as much in the context as the attention drawn to them by the alliteration would suggest? Does it not seem as though the choice of those particular words has been dictated less by a concern for precision and rightness than by a preoccupation with alliteration and internal rhyme? To me, at any rate, they seem little more than gestures towards a desired illusion of portentousness. A further source of the lack of conviction one feels behind the lines is a certain rhythmic awkwardness and inexpressiveness.

The argument requires no gloss. In elaboration, it may be said that "shameless opportunism" is elsewhere exhibited in the poem's mixing of attitudinal modes and assumption of echoes. The gratuitous taking on of a bardic grace note from Dylan Thomas—"and I/ The Adam sinless in our beginning"—is but another instance of Auden's willingness to operate with no disciplined sense of what the poem is organized to receive.

The passages from "A Christmas Oratorio" are selected by Lienhardt to show the kind of confusion to which Auden is susceptible even "when it comes to treatment of clearly defined moral issues—in this case the theme of the Nativity, with comments by a Narrator who is, presumably, the detached observer of the action, pointing the moral but by no means adorning the tale." Lienhardt goes on:

There is no place here to quote examples of his lapses of taste, his lack of proportion which makes him self-important when he wishes to be serious, frivolous or even nasty when he wants to be witty. His values, uncertain and unsystematized, represent nothing appreciably solid or coherent. This subject, if it is to be treated tolerably, demands either genuine simplicity or genuine sophistication in the artist. The poet who writes the two passages quoted has neither qualification. For it is in just the irresponsible spirit, of undefined but "unique" adventure, that he approaches his material.

Would it be fair to say that Leavis and his colleagues are in general disposed to reject the cultivation of adventure in the literary work? We have already cited Leavis's definition of the living principle as a "concrete something apprehended but indefinable." The *Scrutiny* critics reject Auden because his poems betray a misconception of the concrete. The poet thinks to control the poem by asserting a confidence that is nowhere validated in his deployment of materials. His sense of adventure is, in Leavis's terms, adolescent because it is whimsical and irresponsible. Where Leavis demands a disciplined movement toward the indefinable, Auden gives us an expansiveness without determinate function or calculable scope. The result, for the reader of Auden's verse, is a sense of inconsequence and triviality.

We said earlier that Auden is the kind of poet who might have been expected to appeal to Leavis. And had he done, more consistently, what his powers led readers to expect, Leavis would surely have come around. Even in the brief uncharitable reviews there are grudging concessions, including an aside to the effect that "September 1st, 1939" might be exempted from the general dispraise. In the end, the objection central to all the others has to be the sense of inauthenticity and shallowness. The poised knowledgeableness simply overrides, in Leavis's reading, all the strengths and occasional felicities. Auden lacks all conviction; he pretends to know almost everything to conceal—from himself and others—the sorry fact that he luxuriates in his confusion. This is the judgment passed. In reaching his judgment, Leavis does not take the trouble to exempt, in a sustained or serious way, Auden's successful poems. Had he focused on "In Praise of Limestone," "The Shield of Achilles," or several others, Leavis would have had to make substantial adjustments in his appraisal. He refused to make conclusive adjustments, no doubt, because Auden did not in any case seem equipped to do for us what we needed. The technical equipment was there, to be sure, and the command of a sophisticated modern idiom. There might even have been a certain natural piety, a feeling for the commonplace, that ought to have ensured a sincerity of response to the disorder treated in the verse. What was lacking was a clear grasp of what needed to be done, a truly critical appreciation of what values might have been evoked by way of effectual opposition to the aimless drift of contemporary urban life. These are not, as Leavis has them, extraliterary imperatives. They bear upon his sense of what we value in a poem or novel. Had Auden better understood the origins of the natural piety he occasionally felt, he might have understood as well the terrible absence to which his poems everywhere bear witness.

We find in Auden, as in many of the more gifted writers of our day, an incapacity to distinguish better from best and to drive the self toward a positive reverence for what is genuinely good. What Leavis bemoans is the failure to work in the shadow of ideal values by which current feeling and practice may be amply judged. This is not a matter of specific moral truths that the poet is required to affirm. A truth in literature is necessarily apprehended as a counter, which is to say, in relation to what it is not. Its rightness is determined by that relation, by the degree in which it effectively answers the presented situation to which it responds. Where it is most persuasive it will convey no sense that the conflict

47

in which it participates has been definitively resolved. The ideal, such as it is, takes its force from the fact that it is shaped in part by necessity, by a living situation that is unstable and, in many ways, intractable. Ideal values are not so much stated as gestured toward. They have their own necessity in a response to experience that is itself a little unstable, less than willing to be swept off its feet by the given dispensation of the hour. They bear, always, the fine marks of a resistance mounted and sustained. If Leavis objects to the "well-bred innocence" and "sweet, limpid solemnity" of Arnold's verse,[36] as he objects to Auden's peculiar complaisance, he does so in the name of an ideal which requires to be more strenuously and particularly intimated.

But, it may be plausibly asked, what would an ideal value look like in a work of literature, and what resemblance would it have to "real life"? As often in such matters, we can answer more confidently in the negative. Auden's limestone landscape, for example, desirable though it seems to the speaker of his poem, is clearly a diminished thing by the standards to which the poem insufficiently gestures. What makes for the deficiency, even in so fine a poem as Auden's, is the poet's failure to acknowledge with any fullness of response the ideal that stands somewhere in the precinct of his immediate conception. What is required is a tacit knowledge[37] ever so different from the knowledgeableness typically exhibited. A tacit knowledge would know how to intimate that the pleasures and civil graces of a "limestone" universe fall far short of what a large heart might decently desire. A poem built on such knowledge would, in turn, put proper

36. In *New Bearings in English Poetry*, p. 19.
37. A term proposed by the philosopher Michael Polanyi, whose work has meant a great deal to Leavis over the last fifteen years. For references, see *Nor Shall My Sword*.

stress not merely on what it had learned to live with, but on what it had not the strength or conviction to actively desire. Auden's poem succeeds in the degree that it acknowledges alternate dispensations even as it cultivates its "limestone" satisfactions. But the success is slighter than it might have been had the alternate dispensations themselves been figured in the light of their relation to an ideal.

Ideal values, then, are real insofar as they condition what we feel and say about our experience. For the poet they constitute a warrant of authenticity; they signal his awareness of conflict in the very fabric of those adjustments he is pressed to make to get along in the world he inhabits. Where the ideal values come from is an issue of some dispute, though an issue that needs all the same to be confronted. For there is some real sense in Leavis that the possibility of ideal values in literature may be compromised by the culture in which a writer works. This is not to say that writers may not be held responsible for the values generated in their work but that their values may owe something to a living community. Consider: "it is only in the existence of an educated public, capable of responding, and making its response felt, that 'standards' can be there for the critic to appeal to."[38] Or: "The community to which Jonson as a poet belongs is. . . . predominantly ideal. . . . The community to which Dryden belongs as a poet is that in which he actually lives, eats and talks, and he belongs to it so completely, and with its assurance of being sophisticated and civilized. . . . that he has no ear, no spiritual antennae, for the other community."[39] Which is to show that Leavis has consistently argued the importance of the community in considering

38. "There Is Only One Culture" in *Nor Shall My Sword*, p. 98.
39. *Revaluation*, p. 32.

the health and future prospects of literature. That the relevant communities may be actual or ideal may be less important than the fact that they may be appealed to for better or for worse. Dryden, Leavis tells us, had access to community standards that were all too actual, too explicit and confident. But he would not have been better off without such standards to negotiate. The emphasis in Leavis is on Dryden's belonging so completely to his community that he could gain no distance from it. The ideal values to which the great writer is necessarily committed may be cultivated even in a culture whose allegiances are narrower than those of another age.

The relation of community to ideal values is notoriously subject to dispute. So much is this the case that Mrs. Q. D. Leavis has written an essay on Edith Wharton that in several particulars challenges the understanding enforced in her husband's work.[40] One would not think to make so much of this if the Leavises had not so consistently joined forces to make the essential discriminations. Even in the strange matter of Dickens, husband and wife have written almost as one, for many years deriding him as an immature entertainer, later installing him, together, as the central force in the tradition of the English novel. That Mrs. Leavis should have written of Wharton as she does indicates how difficult are the issues relating to ideal values and their implicit presence in works of literature. We can only regret that Leavis did not himself respond in print to his wife's essay, for he might then have been forced to confront one or two questions he has missed—unintentionally, to be sure.

Mrs. Leavis makes a case for Wharton as a first-rate novelist whose gifts were adequate to every purpose but

40. All references here are to "Henry James's Heiress: The Importance of Edith Wharton" (1938), reprinted in *A Selection from Scrutiny*, 2:124–36.

the production of great books. "What makes a great novelist?" she asks. "Apparently not intelligence or scope or a highly developed technique." Though Wharton "had a more flexible mind" than George Eliot and was "better able to enter into uncongenial states of feeling," though she had the special "genius" to diagnose her culture "from the outside" and to "plot its curves contemporaneously, as Jane Austen surely could not," Eliot and Austen are the great novelists, while no one would claim as much for Wharton. Not that the novels fail individually to repay our attention. Her best writings are said to have "permanent worth," and *The Custom of the Country* can with no qualification or embarrassment be called her masterpiece. "What, then, is the problem?" Mrs. Leavis writes: "I think it eventually becomes a question of what the novelist has to offer us, either directly or by implication, in the way of positives." She goes on:

> In *Bunner Sisters, Summer*, and some other places Mrs. Wharton rests upon the simple goodness of the decent poor, as indeed George Eliot and Wordsworth both do in part, that is, the most widespread common factor of moral worth. But beyond that Mrs. Wharton has only negatives, her values emerging, I suppose, as something other than what she exposes as worthless. This is not very nourishing, and it is on similar grounds that Flaubert, so long admired as the ideal artist of the novel, has begun to lose esteem. It seems to be the fault of the disintegrating and spiritually impoverished society she analyses. Her value is that she does analyse and is not content to reflect. We may contrast Jane Austen, who does not even analyse, but, having the good fortune to have been born into a flourishing culture, can take for granted its foundations and accept its standards, working within them on a basis of internal relations entirely. The common code of her society is a valuable one and she benefits from it as an artist. Mr. Knightly's speech to Emma, reproving her for snubbing Miss Bates, is a useful instance: manners there are seen to be based on moral values. Mrs.

Wharton's worthy people are all primitives or archaic survivals. This inability to find any significance in the society that she spent her prime in, or ability to find "significance only through what its frivolity destroys", explains the absence of poetry in her disposition and of many kinds of valuable experience in her books. She has none of that natural piety, that richness of feeling and sense of a moral order, of experience as a process of growth, in which George Eliot's local criticisms are embedded and which give the latter her large stature. Between her conviction that the new society she grew up into was vicious and insecurely based on an ill-used working class, and her conviction that her inherited mode of living represented a dead end, she could find no foundation to build on.

The argument represents the judicial procedure at its best, scrupulously comparative and flexible without flinching from the requirement to say something that will serve to place Wharton in a final way. This is the testing kind of value judgment Leavis has demanded of criticism. But what is the essential burden of Mrs. Leavis's case? That Wharton has only negative values to offer; that insofar as there is positive significance in her work, it must be represented as something that no longer actually exists. This is to say that the analytic gift exhibited by Wharton is a lesser thing than the sort of "poetry" we find in Austen. A great work of literature must take its primary direction from a set of cultural assumptions and standards that may be said to impress itself favorably upon enlightened citizens. The commitment to analyze and "expose" is, in this view, narrowing, and a novel may rely too heavily on what is merely implicit for any genuine sense of positive value to emerge.

Mrs. Leavis's argument doesn't concern itself with distinctions between ideal and actual values, but it should. For to speak only of negative and positive values is to obscure essential discriminations. Mrs. Leavis contends that "the common code of (Austen's) society is a valuable one," but that does not tell us why Austen should have made good use of it while others in her culture did not. Austen might well have belonged so completely to her culture, subscribing so totally to its assumptions, that the "spiritual antennae" Dryden lacked might well have been denied her as well. The common code of Austen's society was valuable only insofar as intelligent persons could without grave misgiving subscribe at least to some of its recommendations. Wharton's society, apparently, lacked such a code, forcing the novelist to diagnose the absence without acquiescing in standards her intelligence could not support. Why Wharton should not then have been able to provide implicit values recommended to her by her considerable personal experience Mrs. Leavis doesn't explain. And she has said, after all, that positives in a novel may be offered "either directly or by implication." Her contention, though, is that Wharton can bring herself to offer them neither in the one way nor the other.

So great is her admiration for Wharton, for her "strength of character" and "inflexible literary conscience," that Mrs. Leavis blames her "faults" on "the disintegrating and spiritually impoverished society she analyses." There is nothing quite like this in any of F. R. Leavis's criticism, and it is important that we understand here a basic difference in emphasis. I do not think that Mrs. Leavis could bring herself to say, with her husband, "that 'social' is an insidious word."[41] She may agree that the word is liable to misuse, and worse, but the approach to literature exemplified in the essay on Wharton stresses just the sort of social influence Leavis has been assiduous to "play down." For it is his contention that the general

41. See "The Responsible Critic" (1953), reprinted in *A Selection from Scrutiny*, 2:280–303.

context in which poems and novels take shape is something too obscure to be much help in accounting for them. Obviously, the work itself indicates some of what may be said about the general situation in which it was written. Wharton's books tell us much of what we need to know about the culture she analyzed. But the critic may not assume that what may be said about society adequately accounts for the work at hand. In blaming Wharton's faults on the society she was forced to engage, Mrs. Leavis mistakes her own postulates for the realized data the critic ought to treat.[42]

It may be that Wharton was victimized by her society in the way that Mrs. Leavis suggests. The point is, we do not know that this was so, and in any case, the novels might have been very different had Wharton confronted those social circumstances in a different way. Mrs. Leavis would never think to claim total social control of an artist so independent and intelligent as Wharton. We cannot really say why she should explain the writer's lack of natural piety by referring so emphatically to the determining social setting.

The several issues developed in the essay on Wharton are crucial for any comprehensive study of Leavis. But it is the community's relation to the values expressed in literature that chiefly concerns us here. Leavis has warned against responses that lose touch with the immediate experience of the work. Yet he wants as well to bring to bear on that experience whatever he thinks relevant. Community standards may be, in this view, a relevant consideration. In what way may community standards be said to matter? Insofar as they affect the writer's capacity to work in the shadow of ideal values, they constitute a significant factor. In her essay on Wharton, Mrs.

42. Again see Leavis on "The Responsible Critic," esp. pp. 292–93.

Leavis doesn't at all consider the curious way values themselves affect a work. She assumes that, because positive values are not promoted, the reader has no prospect of taking any from his encounter with the text. Perhaps, in Wharton, there *are* no significant gestures in the direction of ideal values. We do not argue the particular case. We do dispute the notion that there may be nothing in the way of positives unless they are explicitly formulated and promoted. That is where Leavis would himself have to challenge his wife's emphasis. There is a community in Wharton's novels. She responds to it by taking it apart. Her analysis depends for the effect it makes upon values which she must have an individual hand in creating. If those values are to seem generally acceptable to her contemporaries, they will need also to have been, in part, taken over from the community that nurtures them. But our reading of Wharton is already a different matter. We are not contemporaries, and insofar as her novels may be said to matter greatly to us, they matter because of her response to an ideal community whose values would be finer than any that might have had general acceptance even in a more splendid age than Wharton's.

Leavis has himself had something to say of positive values, and we have seen how the critique of Auden depends in part on the working out of just that issue. In an essay on American literature,[43] Leavis describes the positive dimension in the work of Henry James: "I am thinking of that drama of critical interplay between different traditions. . . . It transcends the vindication of one side against the other, or the mere setting forth of the for and against on both sides in a drama of implicit mutual criticism. The essential spirit of the drama is positive;

43. "The Complex Fate" in *Anna Karenina and Other Essays* (New York: Pantheon, 1967; New York: Simon & Schuster, Inc., 1969), pp. 152–60.

James is feeling, creatively, towards an ideal possibility that is neither Europe nor America." The passage supplies the necessary corrective to the emphasis developed by Mrs. Leavis. The community to which James responds "is neither Europe nor America." It is a community created by the writer, not out of whole cloth, but out of various possibilities he has taken from his experience of the one place and the other. It would be foolish to assert that the actual communities didn't matter or that they had only an incidental relation to the shape of James's imaginings. But surely they did not matter in a fully determining way. In the end, James was a great writer because he responded to the cultures of his acquaintance without feeling called upon to take sides. He used them to fashion something he could not have found in either. If Wharton failed so to use her experience of what were, roughly speaking, the same cultures, the fault had specifically to do with limitations peculiar to her genius.

The relation between the community and the values it may be said either to encourage or to inhibit is the subject of Leavis's chapter on Pope in *Revaluation*. There Leavis makes a case for Pope that goes beyond anything a nineteenth-century critic might have claimed. Regularity and correctness are accounted for with no accompanying sense that they need to be excused. Pope's strength is a function of his conviction that he speaks for something that truly lives and that requires to be celebrated as only he can celebrate it. He finds in himself no resistance to the community in which he lives, and thinks its standards perfectly splendid. If there are those who do not know how to make the best of their advantage as citizens of the realm, who waste or scorn their privilege, they can be dealt with accordingly—it is no secret that Pope had a power of destructive irony rarely seen in English verse. But that Pope's gifts were generally marshaled to affirm what were the central assumptions of his day we cannot doubt. There is no hesitation in defining the *positives* in Pope, or in noting that they are plainly and explicitly asserted. We have seen, in Leavis's reference to Dryden, how limiting a full commitment to community standards may be. In his discussion of "spiritual antennae" Leavis indicates his preference for a literature that is sensitive to implicit values that lie beyond the codes elaborated by any given culture. The crucial passage on Pope may at first be thought to call these formulations into question:

> . . . the 'correctness' of Pope's literary form derives its strength from a social code and a civilization. With Dryden begins the period of English literature when form is associated with Good Form, and when, strange as it may seem to us, Good Form could be a serious preoccupation for the intelligent because it meant not mere conformity to a code of manners but a cultivated sensitiveness to the finest art and thought of the time.
>
> The Augustans could be so innocently unaware of the conventional quality of the code—it was 'Reason' and 'Nature'—because they were in complete accord about fundamentals. Politeness was not merely superficial, it was the service of a culture and a civilization, and the substance and solid bases were so undeniably there that there was no need to discuss them or to ask what was meant by 'Sense.' Augustanism is something narrower, less fine and less subtle, than what Marvell stands for, but it has a corresponding strength of concentration and single-mindedness.[44]

The passage is troubling on several counts. In what exactly does Pope's strength consist? Leavis speaks of "concentration and single-mindedness" as virtues, though in the chapter on Milton, these are among the "defects" for which he takes the poet to task. Obviously there are accompanying virtues in Pope that make his "concentration and single-mindedness" acceptable to Leavis. At an-

44. *Revaluation*, pp. 76–77.

other point in *Revaluation,* he speaks of Pope's "fineness" of organization and "intensity," of the "tensely flexible and complex curve" of the lines "playing subtly against one another."[45] Which is to say that in Pope single-mindedness is everywhere qualified and strengthened by a tension built into the very fiber of the lines, the most obvious manifestation of which is a constant modulation in the tone of the articulating voice. This Leavis amply demonstrates by quoting and leading us through lines from "Epistle IV, Of The Use Of Riches."[46]

The constant tension and modulation of effect in Pope are qualities that have much to do with our response to the standards he affirms. Leavis frequently reminds us, in the chapters on Pope and the Augustans, that no twentieth-century poet would affirm the values of his culture in a manner so firm and undivided. But if Pope is undivided in his primary allegiances, he is complexly responsive to the culture in its particular manifestations. The mind generates its own obstacles and indirections in an effort to speak of its values in a way that can satisfy a properly demanding intelligence. The poetry continues to matter because it expresses more than "conformity to a code of manners." It represents, as Leavis tells us, "a cultivated sensitiveness to the finest art and thought of the time." That is, it expresses an implicit commitment to the community of arts and letters that has only its temporal sanction in the larger community of ordinary men and women. Pope remains for us a living poet because his work gestures toward values that can only be apprehended by those who are sensitive to *thought*: the disinterested valuation, even of standards devoutly held, implicitly commits the poet to values substantially different from anything he would think to state in his verse.

45. "The Line of Wit" in *Revaluation,* p. 31.
46. See pp. 77–81.

But there are other problems. In what degree is Pope's thought properly analytic? He may be said, of course, to objectify his experience. His inclination to do so has made him seem cold and aloof to readers who want their poetry "inspired" and "hypnotic." Those expectations may be summarily dismissed. Less easy to get around is Leavis's observation that Pope has "no need to discuss ... or to ask what was meant by 'Sense' " and other comparable cultural touchstones. This would seem to indicate that a poet may take more or less on faith the dominant conventions informing his verse. If Pope judges something by the standard of "Sense" he may not be required to ask what "Sense" is supposed to mean. He knows, and his reader may also be thought to know. That is enough. Why it should seem enough to Leavis is clear. The palpable substance of Pope's verse is involved in something that actually exists: "the substance and solid bases (of his culture) were so undeniably there," as Leavis says, that he had no need to attach us to a world of his own devising. Sense, for Pope, is indivisibly related to assumptions that are held in a healthy and positive way. These assumptions are not falsely held as the comparable assumptions in Auden may be; that is, they do not invite the poet to strike poses or to pretend a composure that is at odds with the material of the vision. Nor, and here we think of Milton, do the assumptions prompt Pope so to identify with particular emotions that he cannot manage to stand apart from them. We may not feel disposed to approve the standards Pope affirms, but we can attest to the seriousness and flexibility of mind with which he engages them. If, like Austen, he stands very much within what he takes to be a vital culture, and does not feel compelled to analyze, he wins respect because he does so well what his culture demands. The verse is everywhere involved in the working through of standards and values, in the careful placement and imaginative extension of those values. This is ordinarily an activity of analysis. The thought of Pope and of Austen is largely resistant to the work of analysis because it has so firm a hold on what it takes to be true and on the proper means for the correction of what is false.

As Leavis can say of Augustanism that it is "narrower—less fine and less subtle, than what Marvell stands for"—so we can say that Pope's thought is less muscular, less a matter of impressive *self*-discipline, than the thought of, say, T. S. Eliot. To say as much is to acknowledge that a particular kind of limitation is often a function of another kind of advantage. Leavis is quite right to argue that "the 'correctness' of Pope's literary form derives its strength from a social code and a civilization," but his inability to move us in the way that the greatest poets move us is similarly explained. His attachment to the actual community, though not as total as Dryden's, ensures that there will always be a "period" flavor to the verse, what Leavis calls "a note of provinciality." These are not terms of utter condemnation in Leavis, but they do serve to fashion a judgment that is itself subject to additional discriminations.[47]

This leaves us with one further question: If, as it seems, Pope represents the perfection of a mode of impersonality in literature, what general validity may that mode be said to have? No one knows better than Leavis how peculiar were the several merits of Pope's verse to the period in which he lived. Yet the critic is drawn to the

47. See the comparison between Pope and Byron in "Byron's Satire" in *Revaluation*, pp. 148–53. If Byron appeals to "a generous common humanity" ever so different from anything in Pope, the absence of Augustan "formal urbanity and perfect manners" makes him sometimes reckless and "schoolboy." In all, a provocative appendix to the main argument.

quality of impersonality as to no other in his studies of literature. Again and again, in locating what has greatest weight in a particular achievement, he observes a factor that, in Pope at least, was a function of decided limitations: In Ben Jonson we find "the impersonal urbanity and poise that we feel to be the fruit of his Latin studies";[48] in Wordsworth at his best there is, "as an essential characteristic, an impersonality unknown to Shelley";[49] and in Pound, finally, we note—in the supreme "Mauberley" sequence at least—an "impersonality" that measures the poet's "complete detachment and control."[50] Obviously Leavis's sense of impersonality in literature goes a good deal further than anything that may be taken from a reading of Pope. The best writing, whether it looks like Pope's or Wordsworth's or, for that matter, Joseph Conrad's, will be impersonal. Its impersonality will have only an incidental relation to a community of origin, though it will inevitably suggest a tacit apprehension of values that may be commonly held by persons of conviction. Where it exists, it will make itself felt more or less at once, and will direct critical judgment to discuss the true purposes of the work at hand.

The "theory" of impersonality in literature was of course given its most influential modern formulation in Eliot's early essay on "Tradition and the Individual Talent," an essay he came in time to doubt, though never to repudiate.[51] There is issued the now famous dictum that, "the more perfect the artist, the more completely separate in him will be the man who suffers and the

48. *Revaluation*, p. 24.
49. *Revaluation*, p. 172.
50. *New Bearings in English Poetry*, p. 139.
51. See Eliot's reference to "perhaps the most juvenile" of his essays in the preface to the 1964 edition of *The Use of Poetry and the Use of Criticism* (London: Faber & Faber, 1964), p. 9.

mind which creates."[52] This is not all there is to the theory, but it surely indicates that Eliot would have been well advised to repudiate it when he had the chance in reprinting his early criticism. Leavis is not the only writer to question what Eliot intended in speaking of impersonality in a way that no serious poet can have credited. It is interesting to note that, in Stephen Spender's recent book on Eliot, his view of impersonality is largely dismissed, with nothing in the way of sustained argument—as though no one would today conceivably dispute the matter.[53] Of Eliot's essay, Spender writes: "The poet is looked on here as a depersonalized mind measuring the past monuments and relating to their scale the new work produced, while the tradition is seen as an organization of relations established in the past that adapts itself in an evolutionary way to new conditions through objective procedures taking place in the mind of the living artist." Though literary scholars have lately been much absorbed in the study of the poet's relations with his literary fathers, we are far from affirming any view of "objective procedures" such as Eliot is said to have proposed. Eliot's theory of impersonality, in its representation of the creative mind as a *completely* depersonalized mechanism, may hardly be said to answer to the descriptions worked out by Leavis.

Relations between Leavis and Eliot seem never to have been especially warm. Earlier, we indicated that Leavis increasingly tended to see himself engaged with the poet in a struggle for critical primacy. Attacks on Eliot's theory of impersonality, as upon his critical intelli-

52. The line is quoted in Leavis's "T. S. Eliot As Critic" in *Anna Karenina and Other Essays* (New York: Simon & Schuster, 1969), p. 180.
53. See Spender's *T. S. Eliot* (New York: Viking, 1976), pp. 72–73.

gence generally, are developed in a way that suggests that more is at stake than a particular theory or judgment. Be that as it may, Leavis surely has some priority in treating seriously the impersonality to which Eliot devoted an essay better known than anything Leavis wrote. In fact, as early as 1932, in *New Bearings in English Poetry*, Leavis made the case for Eliot's verse precisely on the grounds that there, at last, we should find "the impersonality of great poetry."[54] It would be difficult to overstate the influence that Leavis's book has had on the study of modernism in the English-speaking countries. It may not be unfair to say that it is the treatment of the impersonality of great poetry that has made the book *useful* in a way that continues to recommend itself to students of Eliot and Pound especially. For what Leavis demonstrates is that the judgment of imaginative literature is made possible by a coming to terms with the realization in language of "a comprehensive and representative human consciousness." This realization is the primary achievement of great literature. To speak of it is to describe, in a way that our experience can affirm, what we mean by impersonality. Eliot is not the only modern writer to have achieved what Leavis so admires, but he may be said to have achieved it in a way that has compelled the critic's interest more fully than the work of any other poet.

The reader will want to examine for himself the many dimensions of Leavis's appropriation of Eliot. Our purpose is served by looking into the use of the word "impersonality," and closely associated terms, to describe and to judge what Eliot has done. Leavis's original discussion of the poet in *New Bearings* comes closer to accepting the "mind that created" / "man who suffered" business than anything he later wrote on Eliot. Here and

54. *New Bearings in English Poetry*, p. 83.

there he is gratefully "reminded" that in dealing with a poem we needn't be bothered by thoughts of actual suffering that may have had a part in its composition. Emphasis is given to the poet who associates himself with a "severe and serene control of the emotions by Reason" and whose poetry is to demonstrate "an athleticism, a *training*, of the soul as severe and ascetic as the training of the body of a runner." [55] Eliot's is said to be a "positive achievement" in the sense that he has something to say and a technique ("The spiritual discipline is one with the poetical") for generating an impression of sincerity. His impersonality is a mode of projection, wherein individual concerns are dramatized rather than stated.

Though Leavis says in the early study that we have in Eliot a complete "transcendence of the individual self," the point is not central to his theme, and there is no grave inconsistency in his later decision to stress the very problematic personal dimension of Eliot's thought. Early and late, the accounts of Eliot's mind are similar. If in his immensely detailed late study of *Four Quartets*, Leavis takes Eliot to task for succumbing to a kind of despair and nullity, the reason given is that Eliot has not properly understood the quality of personal life that everywhere figures in his most ambitious poem. Had Eliot properly acknowledged his participation in an ideal community that has, all the same, "a very present depth" in actual lived time, he might have seen to the bottom of his central convictions: that "there is no such thing as persisting— that is, real—identity," and that, "inescapably confined to a 'sphere of being' where there is no direction and no pattern," ordinary life is "meaningless," change "illusory." [56] This was not the basis for the view of imperson-

55. Quotations from two 1926 essays by Eliot, cited in *New Bearings*, p. 114.
56. See "Four Quartets" in *The Living Principle*, p. 241.

ality Leavis had discovered in *The Waste Land* or *Gerontion*. But the recoil from actual life so unmistakably denoted in the spiritual disciplines recommended by *Four Quartets* may well have been a factor in the early poems as well. The fact that Eliot, in the late work, explicitly asserts his rejection of the familiar "sphere of being" simply indicates what may all along have been implicit in his attraction to a severe and impersonal discipline.

Leavis's work on Eliot shows—among a variety of things—how difficult it is to apply critical value-terms in a consistent and adequate way to different works of literature. No one has more strenuously insisted upon the point than Leavis himself, and though we have contended that it is always worth trying to elaborate general principles, we must agree that principles have little in common with rules. The achievement of impersonality may often be said to identify what is enduring in the greatest works of literature; the achievement may also be said— in some occasions—to accompany a major failure of responsibility to what is proposed as the true business of a given work. In *The Waste Land*, as in *Ash Wednesday*, Leavis argues, the "effort to focus an inclusive human consciousness" succeeded because the poem's peculiar organization allowed for equivocations and dramatic ironies that made it unnecessary to take individual statements "at their face-value."[57] Impersonality was a function of tensions built into the poems in such a way that, though general effects might be negative, positive impulses—religious or otherwise—might simultaneously be registered. Different though they were, both poems could be legitimately described as working by "compensations, resolutions, residuums and convergences."[58] The poems were validly impersonal in demanding of the reader nothing in

57. *New Bearings*, pp. 95, 120.
58. Leavis on *Ash Wednesday* in *New Bearings*, p. 120.

the way of assent to a 'Truth' the poet was himself avid to communicate. Eliot's achievement of a "paradoxical precision-in-vagueness" allowed him to communicate, as Leavis says, "without any forcing." Impersonality was the measure of a technical, a *poetic* organization, that could project the necessity for a particular understanding, in *Ash Wednesday* a set of beliefs, without imposing them.

In *Four Quartets,* Leavis contends, impersonality is a cover for a failure to come to terms with the altogether personal emotions that figure so prominently in the poem's affirmations and denials. Lacking a structure that would relieve the poet of the need to state plainly what is, essentially, a life-denying imperative, the poem offers an impersonality that is nothing more than a steady refusal to countenance ordinary feeling. To say as much does not for Leavis amount to a full dismissal of the poem. In resisting Eliot, he pays "tribute to Eliot's genius"[59] in his own way. He demands of the poem that it achieve an impersonality consistent with its own project. By denying validity to human effort generally and refusing even to consider the personal components of his own insistent renunciations, Eliot may be said to falsify his enterprise. This is not, so far as Leavis can tell, a case of deliberate deception but an essential flaw in a project conceived with "intense earnestness." Impersonality, to constitute a genuine achievement, must be a positive achievement, not an evasion. In "Burnt Norton," Leavis says, the poet is "offering to achieve and confirm his reassuring apprehension of a really and supremely real by creative means." His approach is fundamentally unacceptable because it contradicts its very object: "He is committed to discrediting the creative process he undertakes to demonstrate and vindicate." The impersonality that is nothing but "a per-

59. *"Four Quartets"* in *The Living Principle,* p. 191.

66

sonal plight disguised—and betrayed," and that fails to persuade us that anything personal has been genuinely transcended, is not the critical value we might have expected. Working by "successive analogies" that have much in common with the "compensations" and "convergences" of the earlier poems, Eliot in *Four Quartets* stakes too much on turning them "into firm and pregnant certainties."[60] Such certainties cannot answer to the requirements of the divided soul that speaks with painful equivocation even in Eliot's most insistent propositions. The impersonality Leavis so values in Eliot, as in other writers, is not always easy to define, but it is clear that, in *Four Quartets* at least, it is without the profound and complete *sincerity* that might have made it acceptable.[61]

The subject of impersonality is, of course, too large to be adequately discussed in a summary way, but we have been able to indicate, albeit provisionally, that in the work that matters Leavis has been anything but the rigid dogmatist he has been said to be. His criticism tends to be more sensitive to some standards than to others, it is true, but that is to say only that he has a firm sense of what matters. Perhaps, in almost exclusively considering English-language works, he has unnecessarily limited his range and has been blind to several obvious connections. It may be that he should value impersonality less had he cultivated a more sensitive appreciation of Proust and Kafka. Perhaps his understanding of thought would be different had he tried to measure a Conrad not against Henry James or George Eliot but against later writers who have *thought* in ways very different from anything we find in nineteenth-century English writers. But such

60. Quoted fragments in this paragraph may be found on pages 188–91 of *The Living Principle*.

61. For a more positive analysis of impersonality in literature, see my later discussion of D. H. Lawrence, Part 2, Chapter 2.

observations have only limited validity. Leavis's work is good for most of the goals he assigns. It enables a consideration of literature that is deeply serious and committed to the discrimination of better from best. It demonstrates that what we value in thinking generally is closely related to what we value in books. And it demonstrates that, whatever the essential differences between criticism and so-called creative writing, faculties required for the one are very largely dependent upon faculties involved in the other. For that alone we owe Leavis a debt of thanks.

The central propositions developed in Leavis's writing may not be applied as literary rules in the evaluation of poems or novels. They are valuable primarily in their contexts. All the same, they have already instructed two literary generations in the proper reading of texts, and have provided a necessary pivot for arguments about the role of criticism in the life of culture. In his discussions of impersonality, of thought, of ideal value and community, Leavis has erected a series of standards that may not be set aside. He has made himself an authority figure —the term is used here without ironic intention!—who is subject to the varieties of abuse and revolt typically mobilized in our time to deal with authorities of whatever kind. The resistance to Leavis is not in itself a measure of his greatness, but of the impact his work has had. He has shown that a belief in *value* may be interesting even to those who are anxious to deny value judgment as a legitimate mode of critical apprehension. He has, as it were, thrown down a challenge to a profession most of whose "scholars" have been trained to read for meaning rather than for value. In this, he has insisted that literary study is always properly a mode of criticism, and that criticism is itself a response to life more than a specialist response to accredited texts.

To say that, for Leavis, criticism is a mode of thought

and that its primary object is a response to life is to suggest how naturally Leavis has been drawn to the novel. For if the novel is, as Lawrence said, the book of life, it may be supposed to appeal to just those critical instincts Leavis has wished to elaborate. There is some debate as to just where Leavis may be said to have done his best work. George Steiner, in the most important essay ever devoted to the critic, chooses his work on the novel.[62] Others have preferred the books on poetry, representing as they do the critic's close absorption in the very words and images of texts, his ability to *test* general insights against complex particulars. It is not essential that we make such a choice. Our business is to say how the enterprise of judgment differs when its object is a novel; how the critical intelligence will necessarily locate value and stress deficiency when local texture may not be said to play a dominant role in the management of effects. Leavis's writings on the novel have been deeply influential because they develop the idea of value in ways not perfectly or completely anticipated in the books of the 1930s: *New Bearings* and *Revaluation*. That there is no break in the critical vision may be demonstrated not only by the fact that Leavis has continued to write about poetry quite in the way he did much earlier; full appreciation of his contribution requires appreciation of the books on fiction as a necessary *complement* to the books on poetry.

What follows, then, are two studies in Leavis's criticism of the novel. Each is intended to illuminate how the sense of value is specific to the particular literary encounter; also, how criticism is best seen as an attempt to erect standards enabling an approach to literature that is at once flexible and authoritative.

62. See the long essay on Leavis in Steiner's *Language and Silence* (New York: Atheneum, 1967).

PART II.

LEAVIS AND THE NOVEL

1. Henry James

Leavis has never been able to make up his mind about Henry James. He has placed him firmly in "The Great Tradition" of the English novel, and has pronounced *The Portrait of a Lady* and *The Bostonians* "the two most brilliant novels in the language."[1] But the judgments are everywhere uncertain and unsettling even as they pretend to be firm and perfectly convincing. Though James is routinely conceded to be a major force in the tradition of the novel, though his artistry is such as to have made him a model for others, he is shown to be limited in drastic ways that compromise the larger claims. In the prefatory section of *The Great Tradition* the major novelists are said to be "significant in terms of the human awareness they promote; awareness of the possibilities of life." Surely this can be said of James only in a very qualified sense. Determined to include James, to make of him whatever he can, Leavis is persistently brought up against the demands of his own position and forced to put things in a way he might have wished to discourage in others. Perhaps James merited the superlatives Leavis bestows on some of the novels and tales, but the reader of the criticism will feel that the emphasis is inconsistently managed, and that Leavis doesn't fully understand what he responds to in the novels.

James produced a great many works that scholars

1. *The Great Tradition* (New York: New York University Press, 1963), p. 153.

have conveniently divided into early, middle, and late. The conventional wisdom has it that the late novels—*The Ambassadors, The Wings of the Dove,* and *The Golden Bowl*—together constitute the major phase; earlier items are thought to succeed or fail in ways that have only a little to do with those late works, whatever the superficial similarities in outlook or setting. Leavis turns this wisdom on its head, banishing any privileged notion of a major phase, and pronouncing the late novels failures. In addition, smaller experimental works like *The Awkward Age* and *What Maisie Knew,* long discounted, are exalted as brilliant achievements, and the very early *Roderick Hudson* judged a distinguished book with a "sustained maturity of theme and treatment" far surpassing anything in Dickens or Thackeray.[2] Though sustained attention is properly reserved for "big" books like *The Portrait* and *The Bostonians,* lavish praise is also accorded "minor" works like *Washington Square* and *The Europeans.* In all, an improbable, though not an insupportable sequence of judgments.

What is surprising in a critic of Leavis's conviction is the constant equivocation to which his treatment even of the acclaimed masterpieces is subject. *The Portrait* is the most obvious case in point, for it is the one novel of James that almost everyone seems to approve. Leavis thinks it a great novel, and tells us how good it is whenever he has a chance. Yet he uses it as a foil in the most extended work of comparative analysis he ever wrote, finding it radically deficient in ways he cannot hope to retract when the comparative context is no longer required. In " 'Daniel Deronda' and 'The Portrait . . . ' "[3]

2. The "negative" reflection on Dickens will of course need to be revised for subsequent editions of *The Great Tradition.*
3. A forty-five-page chapter in *The Great Tradition.*

Leavis argues that James couldn't have written his novel without using George Eliot's as a model and, in some sense, an inspiration. Or rather, says Leavis, he couldn't have proceeded without *Gwendolen Harleth*, a novel drawn from *Deronda* that salvages what is enduring in the original and cuts away all that is bad—which is to say, a full half of George Eliot's book. Only a critic of tremendous audacity and imagination would think to cut a major work like *Daniel Deronda* so ruthlessly as Leavis does; but it is more than audacity that prompts Leavis to make a case for the hypothetical *Gwendolen Harleth* by working up a devastating critique of *The Portrait*.

Leavis's treatment of *The Portrait* is so disturbing because it calls into question everything he elsewhere says of the novel, as of other works he seems to admire. We cannot feel we know what he means when he calls *The Portrait* a great book, or speaks of its "inclusive harmony," once we have been impressed by the view that it is deficient in the very "human nature" it wishes to explore. *Gwendolen Harleth* may be, as Leavis says, a better book than *The Portrait*—though I don't think it is. But *The Portrait* cannot be said to fall so far short of its own intended mark that comparison may only be said to strengthen Eliot's "position" and to weaken James's, not unless Leavis gives up entirely the case for *The Portrait* as a great book, and comes around to the view that James was at best a second-rate writer. Cogent and, at times, inspiring as the comparative analysis may be, it may be said in this instance at least to compromise the judicial standard by which Leavis has wished to test his criticism. "Final" judgments that are not supported by the tenor and primary thrust of relevant arguments come to seem incidental, not central, to the business of criticism. Leavis has had a hard time with James because here his instinct to analyze and refine has been at odds with the related imperative to judge and rank.

Leavis writes of James in several different books, referring to him in general essays, devoting entire pieces to *Maisie* and *The Europeans*, and putting him at the very center of *The Great Tradition*. The critical "estimate" is unmistakable in the way it is most explicitly stated: James was a supreme master whose novels should be studied by everyone who cares about literature. It is, in general terms, the customary position on James, a position more or less taken for granted for twenty-five years or more. The student of Leavis will feel, however, that the position matters a good deal less than may be supposed, since it permits discrepant observations in no way necessarily implied therein. The *Gwendolen Harleth* study has to be the major document in our consideration, both for impressiveness and scope, though others would do if called upon. Leavis was after all not averse to using James as a foil in various contexts: in writing of Eliot, of Lawrence, and of Tolstoy, to name but three. No one who has read the work on Eliot can be surprised that Leavis should have written of James's "narrowly provident economy" and "severe limitation in regard to significance," or that "Tolstoy is a different kind of man from James—he is the kind of man the greatest kind of artist necessarily is."[4] If James could not give us everything Leavis might have wanted, the deficiency, such as it was, had something to do with the man himself.

Precisely what the deficiency was Leavis doesn't say, though he is largely persuaded by Yvor Winters's view of James as disabled by a residual puritanism he didn't

4. See the title essay of *Anna Karenina and Other Essays* (New York: Simon & Schuster, 1969), pp. 11–12.

really know how to handle.[5] Thus the "habit of moral strenuousness" unaccompanied by any capacity for truly substantive presentment of issues. The observation allows Leavis to speak of "the inveterate indirectness of the later James," of the "context of hints and apprehensions" that surrounds what sometimes seems an emptiness.[6] Had James been able to state more frankly what at some level must have seemed unsayable—or unthinkable—we should have a better appreciation of issues that so exercise his characters. The criticism, if largely limited to the works of the late James, seems fair enough in light of the labored prose and atmospheric murk. James did have difficulty in saying what he saw, and the testimony of his letters and journals and prefaces would indicate that the difficulty was not restricted to the composition of novels. That the problem may be *explained* by the reference to residual puritanism is an altogether different contention. James did, after all, in *Maisie* and other works, manage to speak quite openly of sexual relations and of various kinds of indecent behavior. He was not at any rate the sort of puritan for whom unsavory matters do not exist, or for whom primal need seems marginal to the ordinary conduct of social life. Insofar as James's late works are to be discussed in terms of disproportion and deficiency, they must be said to suffer not from repression or the withholding of attention from unpleasant material, but from an excessive commitment to a certain kind of complexity. It may be that the verbal surface came to be more important to James than it should have been, but this can only be because he saw there the prospect of refining his insights and plumbing depths as nothing else

5. See the references to Winters in *The Great Tradition*, pp. 10–11.

6. *The Great Tradition*, p. 158.

would allow him to. The so-called habit of moral strenu-ousness had a good deal to attach itself to in James's nov-els; where the presentment of substance seems thin, the deficiency must be located not in a residual puritanism but in James's literary judgment.

If Leavis doesn't tell us what was lacking in James as a man, it is not from lack of trying. "He suffered from being too much a professional novelist," we are told; "he did not live enough." Seeking just the sort of ideal com-munity recommended by Leavis in other contexts, James "had to recognize" that nothing really *there* in Europe or America would do, and so unfortunately became a "para-doxical kind of recluse, a recluse living socially in the midst of society."[7] The speculations are familiar. Max-well Geismar and several other readers have made them the center of generally unfavorable accounts of James.[8] The novelist didn't know what he was talking about be-cause he lacked, quite simply, experience. He made things up. The James who had to grope his way through *The Princess Casamassima* because he had virtually no flesh-and-blood experience of the revolutionary anarchists who people that book is the same groping novelist who writes of "personal" relations among men and women. Leavis has no intention of dismissing James in the blunt and programmatic spirit of a Geismar, but the criticism sug-gests he was frequently moved to think of James in not entirely dissimilar ways.

In the *Gwendolen Harleth* study, Leavis finds that James's presentation of character is, by contrast with Eliot's book, deficient "in reality," in "specificity," and finally, "in consistency." *The Portrait*, whatever its merits, is the work of a man whose "idealizing is a matter of not

7. *The Great Tradition*, p. 163.
8. See Geismar's *Henry James and the Jacobites* (New York: Hill and Wang, 1965).

seeing, and not knowing (or not taking into account), a great deal of the reality." The relevant assumption is that the great novelists, like Tolstoy, idealize in another way. But Leavis doesn't so often speak of idealization in the studies of the novel. He is interested in something rather different, though related, something he tries to get at in the paper on *Anna Karenina* when he speaks of "Tolstoy's normative concern" as an inseparable dimension of "real moral judgment."[9] Tolstoy didn't have to idealize because he had a firm sense of what was good and what was not and could relate his feelings to concrete experiences he could comfortably relate to himself. His concerns were normative in the sense that they led him to ask of human beings in his books only what they might reasonably be expected to do. He had no use for abstract conceptions of justice or propriety in order to pass judgments. Tolstoy was directed by what Leavis calls, in another context, "needs of the representative kind that make an artist major."[10] What troubles him may be said to trouble us all. James was not involved in ordinary life in a comparable way, and so, when he judges, we feel too often that the judgment is based on a too partial grasp of relevant facts. He idealizes by simply leaving out what will not suit the purposes of his project; these purposes, we are given to believe, are sometimes too subtle, too much a function of a formal plan, to accommodate the specificity we demand in novelistic accounts of life.

The Portrait seems to Leavis a great book despite James's patent failure to bring to bear appropriate normative concerns in his presentation of the major characters. In Isabel Archer herself we have someone capable of a "radically ethical judgment" that is "a tribute to the

9. *Anna Karenina and Other Essays*, p. 25.
10. See " 'English', Unrest and Continuity" in *Nor Shall My Sword* (New York: Barnes & Noble, 1972), p. 122.

reality with which James has invested her."[11] But the portrait is, all the same, deficient in being "incomplete and indulgent." Though her sensibility may be said to mature—she does learn to make judgments, as Leavis says—Isabel is not permitted to experience remorse or to undergo "the painful growth of conscience" that we would think appropriate to her experience. She stands throughout too much apart from the judgments she is brought to make. She has, Leavis would say, too much of her creator's support to bring down the sort of "critical and unsympathetic" responses that such a character in her imperfection inevitably deserves. "It is hard to believe," says Leavis, "that, in life, she could be as free from qualities inviting a critical response as the Isabel Archer seen by James." The critical judgment, of course, amounts to a declaration that James is not sufficiently moved by normative concerns to make Isabel what she must be to engage the "real moral judgment" a reader will want to exercise. The criticism is, as it were, from life; Leavis judges the character as if she were, or might have been, an actual person. A novel that encourages us to think of persons must provide for its characters what ordinary experience provides for its actors.

The approach to James on these grounds has been taken up by others and may be found in the observations of hostile critics like André Gide. ("They are only winged busts," says Gide of James's characters.) Eliot's defense of the novelist is entirely to the point: "Done in a clean, flat drawing, each [character] is extracted out of a reality of its own, substantial enough; everything given is true for that individual; but what is given is chosen with great art for its place in a general scheme. . . . The focus is a situation, a relation, an atmosphere, to which the characters pay tribute, but being allowed to give only what the

11. *The Great Tradition*, p. 148.

writer wants. The real hero, in any of James's stories, is a social entity of which men and women are constituents."[12] We note the expression "substantial enough" in Eliot's formulation of the case: James's plan committed him to doing certain things that required selection and simplification. The plan is not itself simple, nor does it invite a simple minded or reductive reading. It does ask that we forgo particular expectations in favor of others. Leavis wants the novel to be substantial in a way that James's plan cannot fully satisfy. He understands perfectly what James intended and respects the writer's absolute sincerity and devotion to his task. He speaks with sympathy of James's "firm plan" which may be said to express "a definitive and masterful purpose and excluding all that doesn't seem necessary in relation to this."[13] The criticism he mounts is a legitimate extrapolation from the central observation, namely, that "addiction to 'art' in this sense entails a severe limitation in regard to significance." We may not agree that significance need be understood as Leavis understands it, but there can be no mistaking the objection. For Leavis, the social entity of which Eliot speaks cannot itself be properly grasped without a fuller and more particular expression of the character types the society may be said to nurture. Clean, flat drawings may be beautiful to look at and altogether admirable in their way, but they are not what we look for in the greatest novels.

It is especially interesting that Leavis should choose to focus the critique of James in a comparative analysis of *Deronda*. Though we have mentioned the audacity of the enterprise we have not yet spoken to the obvious point: that, in his willingness to extract *Gwendolen Harleth* from

12. Quoted in F. W. Dupee's *Henry James* (New York: Sloane, 1951), p. 126. See also p. 125 for references to Gide.
13. In *Anna Karenina and Other Essays*, p. 11.

the novel in which it is set, Leavis makes allowances for Eliot that he seems positively unwilling to make for James. This is no simple matter, to be sure, but it must be stressed that the *Gwendolen Harleth* Leavis admires is not a self-contained entity within a larger whole, but a broken sequence of chapters that alternate with others Leavis rejects as unworthy of George Eliot. Eliot, it is said, had a comprehensive grasp of the realities involved in her novel. When we read it, as when we read the better parts of *Felix Holt*, we are moved to say: "this is human nature, this is the fact and these are the inexorable consequences."[14] Eliot sees too much too clearly to simplify and extract in the way that James's plan requires. The critique structures a comparative judgment that makes of James an indisputably lesser novelist and allows Leavis to conclude with a reference to Eliot's "Tolstoyan depth and reality." It is all really quite amazing, depending as it does for full and final confirmation on one's willingness to value a fragment of a novel and to dismiss the rest as inessential to an appreciation of the project as a whole. Were Leavis to take comparable pains on behalf of James's book, he might come up with a reading no less ingenious, yet a good deal easier to accept without compromising one's sense of the inviolable integrity of the novelistic project. If Eliot may be said to have succeeded in spite of the inert matter we find in *Deronda*, why may not James be said to have tried our patience—in his overly tolerant portrait of Isabel Archer, at least—in the interests of a positive ideal he wished to pursue? Though Leavis never says that novels must conform absolutely to a standard we bring indiscriminately to bear on every one, he seems willing to suspend ordinary judgment only where his sense of life has been satisfied in a particular way. Though he admires James, he judges him almost ex-

14. *The Great Tradition*, p. 57.

clusively by standards that do not always illuminate what James's books may be said to provide.

The critic John Bayley has had much to say of these matters, and, especially in his recent *The Uses of Division*,[15] has spoken cogently about the limitations of Leavis's standards. Significance itself, as a standard, may not be able to get at what matters in a novel. Insistence upon significance, a quality said to be lacking in James as a very condition of his genius, may lead the critic to demand a certain kind of significance at the expense of other kinds equally valued by discriminating readers. Thus, says Bayley, Hardy may not appeal to Leavis only "because of something opaque and baffling in his art." Just so, we may say, Eliot seems more appealing than James because she is so good at evoking what Leavis calls a "system of pressures" that permits the critic to enforce his own sense of the "true" reality with a progressive coherence that is likely to seem persuasive. James, by contrast, gives us more in the way of atmosphere than system. Though the atmosphere, in *The Portrait* at least, is anything but vague, it does not encourage the effort of definition in the way that Leavis would like. Why doesn't James take apart in a more concerted and determined way the American culture that may be said to have produced a romantic and somewhat delusional young woman like Isabel Archer? That is what Leavis wants to know. Such an analysis may not be, strictly speaking, required for the portrait of the lady, but it would necessarily generate a critical perspective that might encourage the novelist to deal more severely with his character. That James did not wish to treat Isabel in this way, thinking to have exposed and punished her innocence enough in subjecting her to a most unhappy fate, does not satisfy the critic.

The issue is so especially difficult to handle because,

15. Viking, 1976.

in his study of James and Eliot, Leavis manages to say useful and original things that go far beyond what anyone else has been able to say. The issue, though, is not whether Leavis is at his best a brilliant and gifted reader. Anyone who has studied him knows what Leavis can do. The issue is the use and persuasiveness of a consistently judicial criticism, here applied to James. Bayley is quite right in suggesting that Leavis's "life" standard may not be legitimately applicable in dealing with certain writers. In stressing Dickens's wholeness, for example, Leavis has to make the novelist into a consistent and organized writer who seems much closer to E. M. Forster, shall we say, than one would suppose who had just read a book like *Little Dorrit*.[16] Of the Dickens who wrote that book it is not appropriate to conclude, as Leavis does, that he or his art was on the side of life. Such an art, says Bayley, "is dramatically in the grip of life itself."[17] Of James we may have to say, not that he was in the grip of life, but that, in *The Portrait*, he was concerned to show to positive advantage what was quite obviously an imperfect approximation of ideal qualities to which no reader would fail to be at least partially committed. The judicial approach fails Leavis in the degree in which it forces him to choose between his own devout admiration of James's achievement (and his related sympathy for Isabel), and his view of "the great novel" as tending to deliver something else.

In a recent book entitled *The Classic*,[18] Frank Kermode discusses some of the very issues to which our considerations have brought us. He does so, in part, by picking a quarrel with Mrs. Leavis, entering objections that have much in common with our critique of Leavis on

16. See Leavis on *Little Dorrit* in *Dickens The Novelist*.
17. See the final chapter on "Dickens and his Critics" in *The Uses of Division*, pp. 90–103.
18. Viking, 1976. See especially pp. 131–34.

James. In "A Fresh Approach to *Wuthering Heights*,"[19] Mrs. Leavis performs just the sort of operation her husband performs in his reading of *Deronda*. She proposes to account for Emily Brontë's success by cutting away parts of the original text. In Kermode's words, the critic identifies a variety of passages of "unregenerate writing," which are "discordant with the true 'realistic novel' we should attend to." Her reading, she claims, "enables us to see Emily Brontë as a true novelist. . . . whose material was real life and whose concern was to promote a fine awareness of human relations and the problem of 'maturity'. And we can't see this unless we reject a good deal of the text as belonging more to 'self-indulgent story.' " Kermode's response to Mrs. Leavis may be called in witness of objections we must make, not only to the treatment of *Deronda*, but of James's work as well. Mrs. Leavis creates, says Kermode, "by a peculiar archaeology of her own," an altogether problematic, which is to say a frankly speculative "hierarchy of elements." What she does not seem to appreciate adequately is "the coexistence in a single text of a plurality of significances from which, in the nature of human attentiveness, every reader misses some—, and, in the nature of human individuality, prefers one." Mrs. Leavis's reading depends upon a view of the classic text as timeless in the qualities that ought to be preserved. She believes she has identified an "essential" *Wuthering Heights* that is unfairly compromised by readings that dwell on the rejected portions. Kermode's view of the classic text, as he tells us, "supposes that the reader's share in the novel is not so much a matter of knowing, by heroic efforts of intelligence and divination, what Emile Brontë really meant. . . . as of responding creatively to indeterminacies

19. In F. R. and Q. D. Leavis, *Lectures in America* (New York: Pantheon, 1969), pp. 84–152.

of meaning inherent in the text." His view does not require that we reject Mrs. Leavis, any more than we need to reject portions of *Wuthering Heights*. He is content to accept that the classic text "might well signify differently to different generations, and different persons within those generations."

Kermode, as it were, draws the line that distinguishes a consistently judicial criticism from the more "open," or plural, or, as he might call it, creatively indeterminate criticism that prides itself on being tolerant of what is indeterminate or divided in the text. By his standard, which may be difficult to dispute because it is not, in Leavis's sense, a standard at all, we are not required to reject Leavis's critique of James. We simply make use of it as best we can. If Leavis seems not to know, finally, precisely what to make of James, he can be counted upon all the same to illuminate his use of symbols, his arrangement of various alternatives within a given context, and his relation to his novelistic predecessors. Our reading of James will be enhanced, our capacity for collaboration enlarged, however we feel about the "testing" judgment that has *The Portrait* so decidedly inferior to *Gwendolen Harleth*.

Leavis does not wish to be read in this way, of course. When he speaks of the great critic's irresistible rightness he means that he intends to be accepted, final judgments and all. Indeed, to reject the placements that together constitute a hierarchy of value is to reject the possibility of ultimately meaningful, which is to say, of impersonal discriminations. If James may or may not be the equal of George Eliot at her best, then we may or may not be said to understand what his novels require of us. To concede that kind of uncertainty where indisputably major figures are concerned is to indicate that we do not know the things that really count. We do not know what constitutes a positive good, or how to identify the sort of indulgence that characterizes an unacceptable habit of thought. Leavis insists we put James next to Eliot, Lawrence, and Tolstoy because only in so doing can we see what may otherwise be obscured by the brilliance of James's writing. The judicial critic demands that we refuse to be "taken in," even by the creative genius of a James.

Leavis doesn't extract a fragment of *The Portrait* from the original text and treat it as an independent whole. He does demand of James that he be a Tolstoyan novelist in a way he cannot possibly have been given to anticipate from the novel itself. The approach to *Deronda* is so frankly speculative and hypothetical that we are hard put to object, much though we feel Leavis has constructed a hierarchy of elements that suits his own critical disposition more than Eliot's; and of course, the *Gwendolen Harleth* Leavis describes is indisputably a better "book" than the wordy, rhetorically inflated, and often absurd "book" on Deronda that Eliot may be said to have joined to it. We object to the treatment of James because Leavis asks the novelist to be what he so clearly was not, and permits himself in the comparative context to make judicial observations that are really unsupportable. James is said to be indulgent. This is supposed to mean that in *The Portrait* he lets himself get away with things too easily, even as he indulges Isabel's wish to be proud in her disaster and to continue to believe in the validity of her independent reflections. That James thought Isabel worthy of the respect he continued to show her—with whatever ironic qualification—doesn't really matter to the critic who wants her to suffer just as Gwendolen Harleth is made to suffer. For Leavis, James's indulgence represents a failure of thought, which is a failure to imagine what such a person as Isabel deserves. James wanted to draw Isabel quite as she appears to us: of this the novel itself persuades us and requires no special testimony from the notebooks or prefaces. Leavis believes it as well. He disputes James's decision on the grounds that it makes for limitations in significance that might not otherwise have been imposed. To understand his objection it may be necessary to consider, briefly, what he once says of George Eliot, culminating a developed argument: "George Eliot sees too much and has too strong a sense of the real (as well as too much self-knowledge and too adequate and constant a sense of her own humanity) to be a satirist."[20] That is to say, the Tolstoyan novelist will not be content to take people lightly, even if it seems to him that they do not suffer from being so taken, and the tone of the work in which they appear may best be managed by refusing to make them more impressive than they need to be. By "impressive," of course, we may mean not only grand or audacious, but impressive in the expressed range and depth of suffering. Why the satirical should seem fundamentally unworthy to Leavis when he speaks of Eliot and James we cannot say, but the determining bias is clear.

James's indulgence extends, in Leavis's account, to other portraits as well. In the late novels one character after another is said to disappoint: Strether in *The Ambassadors* is too tolerantly allowed to work himself up over a failure we cannot really identify; *The Golden Bowl* invites us to accept the Ververs in the only way possible, which is in fact impossible: by "forgetting our finer moral sense—our finer discriminative feeling for life and personality"; and so on. As far as they go, the critiques of the late novels warrant serious consideration, or so they seem to me. The study of *The Portrait* is more troubling, even on the question of indulgence that Leavis had

20. From *The Great Tradition*, p. 91.

handled so brilliantly in his studies of the tradition in poetry. He convinces us rather easily that James's Osmond is a *version* of Eliot's Grandcourt. He goes on to make us wonder what he can possibly mean by stressing the inexplicitness of James's portrait by contrast with Eliot's more concrete and vivid presentment of Grandcourt. The negative value-term in Leavis's discussion is *suggestive*: what is suggestive is a matter of mere "overtones," of shadow without substance, of "glimpses from a distance."[21] Can Leavis possibly be speaking, if only by contrastive implication, of Gilbert Osmond? But Osmond is so patently not a matter of shadowy implications that we come to feel his intimate presence in the book almost with the shudder of pained apprehension Isabel is persistently said to experience. That he is something of the stock conspirator of European melodrama does not compromise the detail in which his character is observed. We may not be able to read his exact facial expressions in just the way Leavis would recommend, but we can recite the catalog of his abuses and self-deceptions as if they had been a daily fact of life. Nor is the presentment exclusively a matter of generalized authorial observation and atmospheric contrivance. We see him, intensely, as Isabel sees him and thinks of him; and we see him from the perspective of others, like Ralph Touchett, who have some real sense of what he's worth. Nothing in James could be less "indulgent"; indeed, if we really have to speak in contrasts, we know a good deal more about Osmond, particularly about how he came progressively to be the man he is, than we do of Grandcourt's progress. And it isn't James who indulges a fanciful desire to have done with his beastly character by shuffling him off, thereby freeing Isabel to show what she can do with the experience she's had. Leavis might have reminded himself that, by

21. See *The Great Tradition*, p. 114.

contrast, it is Eliot who willfully breaks the spell in which her princess is held, killing off Grandcourt in a most implausible and unsatisfactory way—whatever the vividness of Gwendolen's subsequently enacted horror and remorse.

Though Leavis thinks *The Portrait* one of the most brilliant novels in the language, he is uncomfortable with it in a degree that would seem to dispute his own judicial valuation. His criticism, moreover, has tended on various occasions to rely on James to bring out the comparative strengths of other writers great beyond his means. This we have seen. Though valuing the ethical dimension of James's work, Leavis has in part rejected the novelist's effort to pose ethical problems "in a pure state," as Winters says, to define them "in their essence, as pure imperatives and commitments."[22] The rejection has not always been as clear and consistent as Leavis would like to think, and the student of the criticism will want to ask questions beyond anything we can manage here. What, for example, do we make of Leavis's valuation of *The Europeans* as a "masterpiece of major quality" which calls in question the critical tradition that sets too high an estimate on "the 'creation of real characters' " and other comparable achievements? Leavis's insistence on an "adult criterion of point and relevance in art" would seem to propose just the simplification and essentializing that James does so well in *The Portrait*. Nor does Leavis treat *The Europeans* as something altogether different from the novels he typically discusses. For him, it invites comparison with works like *Roderick Hudson* and *The Bostonians*. The selectiveness of applied, or discovered, criteria is more than enough to give us pause, when we think of the very different

22. See Peter Brooks, "Henry James and the Melodrama of Consciousness," in *The Melodramatic Imagination* (New Haven, Conn.: Yale University Press, 1976), p. 159.

standards evoked in discussion of *The Portrait*. But it is not *The Europeans* that seems most interesting for our purposes. Because it seems to me so much less than the masterpiece Leavis applauds, it ought not to be allowed to test judgment of James in any final way; I should be too disposed from the first to dispute Leavis's reading. Our project is better served by brief consideration of *What Maisie Knew*. This book seems to me every bit as good as Leavis contends, though it is worth asking whether he arrives at a conclusive judgment in fully appropriate ways.

Maisie can hardly be said to be everyone's favorite James novel. Bayley finds Leavis's admiration for the book "incomprehensible," and an earlier critic like Spender can speak of the book as "obscene." It is, to be sure, a strange and disturbing book, written in the late style but without the corresponding architectural variety and amplitude we find in a work like *The Wings of the Dove*. Leavis admires chiefly the book's patient development of an ideal of moral genius, embodied in a character perfectly capable of affirming positive values. However it may be lacking, in whole or in part, in other more or less successful James novels, "the normative concern with a concept of an essential human goodness" is everywhere apparent in *Maisie*. This is the burden of the important essay on *Maisie* Leavis wrote to flesh out the fragmentary insights offered in *The Great Tradition*.[23] Curiously, Leavis does not seem to care very much about the relation of the late style to the total *experience* of *Maisie*, though he has much to say about just that relation in discussions of other late works. That the novel "does certainly demand of the reader a close and unrelaxed attention, an actively intelligent collaboration" he can say, without enquiring

23. "*What Maisie Knew*" in *Anna Karenina and Other Essays*, pp. 75–91.

into the nature of the collaboration specifically required.[24] The normative concern that so distinguishes *Maisie* would seem to have invited a reasonably close and technical enquiry, for concern is expressed in a language that obstructs substantive appropriation of the kind we expect in most novels.

"The trouble with the late style," Leavis has written, "is that it exacts so intensely and inveterately analytic an attention that no sufficient bodied response builds up: nothing sufficiently approaching the deferred concrete immediacy that has been earned is attainable."[25] The description would seem to suit *Maisie* as well as the other late novels. *Maisie* does defer certain kinds of immediacy in a way that may promise more than James can bring himself to provide. The entire novel may be described as an intricate series of deferrals and desperate reticences. And it does, of course, exact precisely the analytic attention that Leavis elsewhere defines and extols. Why, then, should the critic admire *Maisie,* and how does he account for the emergence of a genuine normative dimension from a book that might have seemed unpromising?

The essay on *Maisie* contrasts the novel with the more popular *The Turn of the Screw,* in a way that has seemed acceptable to most subsequent critics of James. Though there is an air of uncertainty in *Maisie,* though the unspoken frequently hangs between characters with an awful threat, we do not feel the book to be primarily a matter of atmosphere. In *The Turn of the Screw* we have, by contrast, "a mere thriller" with "no ponderable significance." That is to say, though *evil* would seem to be involved in the novel, it may be said to have had "no particular significance for James." No particular significance —evil may have a part to play in affecting reader response

24. See *The Great Tradition*, p. 156.
25. *The Great Tradition*, p. 168.

and working up suspenseful emotion, but it will not affect anyone's estimate of human nature or ordinary relationship. In *Maisie* there is a vision of human possibility informing every reticence and obstruction; in *The Turn of the Screw* there is mystery without determinate content or point. Whatever the tangle of language and the almost impossible intricacy of plotting, *Maisie* has something to say, and the fully attentive reader will be gratified to discover what it is. The reader who prefers *The Turn of the Screw* will be satisfied with the sort of "calculating contrivance" we think of when we mention Poe. Leavis is perfectly willing to call it a triumph without conceding that it ought to be discussed in the way one discusses James's fully serious work.

Maisie, then, is distinguished not only by normative concerns but by its capacity to make us feel that it deals in something real despite the unwillingness of characters —including Maisie herself—to call it by a rightful name. It is analytic in demanding that every item of consciousness be earned and accounted for, even when it cannot be exactly articulated. What it exacts from us by way of analytic attention it earns by taking nothing for granted, by reproducing in vivid detail the process by which one thought manages to join another or to enlarge its potential grasp of objects in its field of vision. In fact, though Leavis doesn't think to get at *Maisie* in this way, the novel may be said to provide a case study in the dynamics of vision. If it affirms positive values in an acceptable way, it does so by discovering those values progressively, rather than imposing them from without. A recent critic of the novel, Alan Spiegel, relates James's procedure to the "strategy of search and seizure": we get, in *Maisie*, not only a painstaking demonstration of how the "eye tracks down its object and takes full possession of its meaning," but an experience of what it feels like to think critically. As James "translates the object (including events, random insights and intuitions) into a function of analytic discourse and speculation," the reader is pressed to accomplish comparable critical operations of his own in order to follow Maisie's thought. When Leavis speaks of Maisie's prodigious powers of discrimination he ought to consider, as Spiegel does, why a reader should be moved to believe in those powers. Quoting an extensive passage from the text of the novel, Spiegel shows what is primary in James's mode of presentment: the dramatic action that looms so large in *Maisie* is itself indistinguishable from the protagonist's "cognitive experience"; we believe in Maisie's growing powers because we watch them grow and participate with her in the difficult negotiation of obstacles that lie in the way of her understanding and ours. The novel's central "search" is "the observer's slow, tentative, often erratic but ineluctable motion from the state of apprehension to the state of comprehension."[26] Leavis responds so warmly to *Maisie* because he feels that it gives us something we don't have to make up all by ourselves, in the absence of determinate content. He speaks of discriminations and values and concealments, and they are all to the point. But he might better have described the novel as an exemplary instancing of the process of thought. He would then have told us that what *Maisie* gives us is more than any particular affirmation; it gives us, after all, nothing less than a mind, and a pregnant intimation of depths and devices to which any mind may have recourse.

Like other critics, Leavis stresses the moral understanding Maisie comes miraculously to develop in cir-

26. See Alan Spiegel, *Fiction and the Camera Eye* (Charlottesville: University of Virginia Press, 1976), especially pp. 54–58. The study contains brilliant analyses of Conrad, Joyce, and Flaubert, among others.

cumstances so squalid that no one around her can quite make her out. What makes his discussion of the novel so fine, despite his failure to address very central issues, is his insistence that Maisie may not be equated with the stereotyped innocent victims of several standard Victorian fictions—including thrillers like *The Turn of the Screw*. Her goodness is not a negative virtue depending on her pitiful subjection to the devices of others. She is, almost alone in the circumscribed universe she inhabits, a moral agent whose capacity to confront what is done to her and to resist—within her means—is a function of thought. She is no intellectual, but she takes imaginative possession of her situation with a firmness and penetration that indisputably recommend her intelligence. Leavis, again, doesn't stress the dimension of thought in *Maisie* as he should in accounting for the novel's power, but he understands perfectly the way her thinking works. Does Maisie lie for the adulterous lovers that surround her— lie, as the critic Marius Bewley wrote, "valiantly, scrupulously, innocently"? Leavis argues that she does not, that it is only a critic's "attempt at assimilating Maisie to the children of *The Turn of the Screw*" that could make him think so. For Maisie, we are told by James himself, "concealment had never necessarily seemed deception," and the "pacific art of stupidity" she is said to practice is anything but innocent. Leavis quotes a key passage from the opening of the second chapter of *Maisie*. It begins with reference to "the complete vision, private but final, of the strange office she filled." The vision is described, moreover, as "literally a moral revolution accomplished in the depths of her nature." James goes on:

> She had a new feeling, the feeling of danger, on which a new remedy rose to meet it, the idea of an inner self or, in other words, concealment. She puzzled out with imperfect signs, but with a prodigious spirit, that she had been a

centre of hatred and a messenger of insult, and that everything was bad because she had been employed to make it so. Her parted lips locked themselves with the determination to be employed no longer.

Leavis discusses the child's resolve in terms of a judgment that, for all the conflicts that occasionally bring it to temporary irresolution, "never loses." Which is to say, Maisie is precisely the sort of judge upon whom the prospect of a civilized future depends. She is representative in falling before experiences to which she is temporarily unequal, but in time she masters experience through a process of thought the novel is everywhere assiduous to evoke. She practices concealment as an art in the sense that it enables what seems a disinterested valuation of persons and behaviors brought before her. We know, of course, that at bottom her art is anything but disinterested, that it implicitly expresses a felt need which can be satisfied only by remaining implicit. James posits a necessary relation between concealment—the refusal to say or to show what one is experiencing—and the "idea of an inner self," and Leavis approves the equation. Its validity is persuasive in the degree that we believe the self has a content that is worth preserving and that is somehow lost in contact with others. The danger Maisie feels is the prospect of absorption into a world of others for whom nothing is true. In such a world, the capacity to discriminate and to judge is of no value, for one thing can be made to seem just like every other, even as persons exchange sexual partners and role functions with no thought of definition or commitment. Maisie preserves an inner self in the face of persistent pressure to "innocently" acquiesce in the promiscuous behavior of her elders. Her inner self, such as it is, resists the pressure, and her capacity to discriminate and to judge grows accordingly.

Leavis would seem, then, to be drawn to *Maisie* for a variety of reasons that bear upon his own work as a critic. The novel may be said to demonstrate the kinds of pressure to which persons may plausibly be subjected and the necessary means by which resistance becomes effectual. The importance of Maisie's judgment for Leavis suggests she may mean more to him than she may to others. Perhaps she doesn't fully exist in the sense that other memorable characters in nineteenth-century fiction do, but that would seem to be almost beside the point. Her thought exists as a palpable something with an unmistakable relation to objects in the world. If those objects have a life that depends almost entirely upon their capacity to exercise Maisie's reflections, they may yet be said to matter to us as "independent" objects in fiction rarely can. Maisie's judgment is so wonderful a faculty because it does not require the constant verification of what Bayley calls "corrective verisimilitude," a significant factor in the work of writers like Trollope and George Eliot.[27] So entirely does the prose texture of the novel represent the alternating forward momentum and retraction of Maisie's thought that our sense of her judgment is of something that has indisputably made contact with the quick of its experience. Leavis's demand that the work of art give us thought and analysis and discrimination, that it invite collaborative engagement and an affirmation that will be the final expression of moral judgment, is incomparably answered by *Maisie*.

But there is more to say. The normative dimension that Leavis locates in *Maisie* is a concern for a standard of "essential human goodness." That standard is significant to us because it is persistently tested in the very marrow of the book's unfolding. We feel that Maisie is good not in the sense that we should like to know her or,

27. See Bayley in *The Uses of Division*, p. 100.

somehow, to take her as a model. We experience good-ness as an implicit standard in terms of which Maisie rejects what she is offered. That Maisie cannot really say what that standard is can compromise it only for a char-acter like James's Mrs. Wix, who knows what she knows and has no patience for refinements and subtleties. Mrs. Wix is, in the world of James's novel, good enough, but hardly what Leavis means when he speaks of the book's positive values. For Leavis, positive values are earned or they are not positive. Their affirmation is a result of a strenuous combat in which life instincts win out over what is barren or negating. Maisie moves us because she has to struggle to win. After a while, her judgment is no longer in doubt—she is capable—but the intricacy of the situation she is asked to master becomes ever more daunt-ing. It is a tribute to James that, compelling though the novel is as a testing of Maisie's critical faculties, and of our own collaborative dexterity, we never feel that we have "left the realm of morals for that of epistemol-ogy."[28] The discriminations Maisie achieves, and the judgments they enable, are valuable not alone because they represent a feat of penetration and intelligence, but because they are in the service of something we take to be good. We feel, are made to feel, in reading *Maisie*, that the force of intimation is ever so much more important than the quantity of deferred concrete immediacy Leavis misses in the late novels.

And what, after all, may we be said actually to miss in *Maisie*? The Leavis who found George Eliot too re-alistic and self-aware to be a satirist is quite content to think of *Maisie* as a "witty and satirical" novel in the mode of "an extraordinarily high-spirited comedy." That he can also speak of its moral "squalor" suggests that it registers effects upon him in a very complex way. What

28. Dupee, *Henry James*, p. 193.

he would seem to indicate is that the book doesn't give us leave to expect the sort of concrete immediacy we look for in *The Portrait*. There, in spite of a persistent undercurrent of qualifying irony, and some broad satirical effects—largely directed at secondary characters—we feel that something we positively require is withheld from us. The comedic effects, as it were, betray an incapacity to engage materials with the fullness they obviously deserve. Dupee, in his way, corroborates Leavis's impression when he describes Isabel Archer's adversities as "more symbolic than experiential" and speaks of moral intelligence in James's heroes as too often "taken for granted": they are, as he says, "imperfectly tempted."[29] Maisie is by contrast genuinely and persistently tempted. If she doesn't actually know what indiscriminate sexual coupling feels like to the persons so involved, she has certainly a good idea of what it costs them by way of the calculation, deception, and waste of spirit to which they are necessarily committed. And of course, it is not sexual activity as such that tempts Maisie, but participation in the forms of promiscuous indifference and cold connivance that make possible a certain kind of sexual behavior.

Leavis insists that sex, in *Maisie*, "is only marginal to James's preoccupation" and must be so as "an essential condition of the kind of poignant comedy" he aimed at. This is to acquiesce in the conventions of genre in an all too explicit and limiting way, I should say.[30] The poignant comedy James wrote did not absolutely require the relegation of sexual concern to a marginal status in the economy of the novel. It required merely that Maisie's sense of what she knew be implicit, and that novelistic approximations to the thing itself remain oblique. Dupee,

29. Dupee, p. 125.
30. See the discussion of Leavis on genre in the Milton section of this study, Part 1.

once again, locates the very heart of James's art in the texture of the language. "Increasingly," he reminds us, "the language [of *Maisie*] rejoices in sudden colloquialism, raffish jargon, and a habit of turning abruptly and alarmingly concrete. . . . Above all, the medium begins to put forth remarkable metaphors without fear of violating its prose character." These metaphors—and there are dozens of examples any reader might select from the text of the novel—introduce, intimate with unmistakable force of affect "the realm of the physical and the elemental, of latent horror."[31] Leavis is mistaken when he argues that "there is no hint here of any moral intensity directed upon sexual misconduct." He wishes, obviously, to protect James against the usual vulgar charge that he was a puritan—a charge brought with considerable regularity against Leavis himself. But what can it mean to say, in elaboration of the point, that "the moral sense that James defines and conveys . . . is that focused in Maisie"? Clearly it is not sexual activity in itself that can be said to figure in Maisie's judgments. She is not herself a devout and colorless little puritan. If she has a moral sense, though, it must be exercised upon something, and that something is surely involved in—though not reducible to—sexual misconduct. The "latent horror" we come to feel in the novel's striking metaphors, the aspect of "the physical and the elemental" that James smuggles in, is a response to the sexually indiscriminate matings of Maisie's elders. That we may be less horrified than Maisie by these activities doesn't blunt the force of the moral intensity James directs upon them by posing them as a dominant object of Maisie's exertions.

Perhaps it would be well to say, in partial extenuation of Leavis's emphasis, that in *Maisie* sexual misconduct is a metaphor for all of the denials of substance

31. See Dupee, pp. 193–94.

and value that call down the judgment we admire. It is nothing so simple as sexual misconduct that we are invited conclusively to deplore. We respond, instead, to a triumphant exercise of discriminative thinking that refuses to accept that one thing is likely to be as good as another, or that making do is a sufficient mode of activity for ordinary persons. Leavis is, finally, quite right to insist that *Maisie* is, in essence, a positive work. It is, in fact, a vindication of critical judgment as few other novels may be said to be.

2. D. H. Lawrence   *Leavis에 대한*

The great English novels are *Sons and Lovers, Lady Chatterley's Lover*, and *Women in Love.*—Simon Lacerous

There was an undergraduate just last week asking me which of Shakespeare's plays he should start with, to work up Shakespeare for his examinations. "Shakespeare!" I said. "Why, man, you haven't even read *The Rainbow* yet! Don't talk to me of Shakespeare until you've gone through Lawrence twice and made a list of everything he has to say against the Establishment."
—Simon Lacerous[1]

LEAVIS has adopted Lawrence in a degree that goes beyond anything we may find in the work of other important critics. Though Frederick Crews's parody makes the critic Lacerous overstate the case, the parody contains more than a little truth. Here are a few statements from Leavis's first book on Lawrence (1955):

It is Lawrence's greatness that to appreciate him is to revise one's criteria of intelligence and one's notion of it.

. . . he was a very remarkable literary critic—by far the best critic of his day.

. . . the plain fact is that Lawrence is one of the great masters of comedy.

One wouldn't, it is true, call Lawrence, any more than one would call Shakespeare, a "stylist"; but he seems to me to be plainly one of the greatest masters of what is certainly one of the greatest of languages.[2]

1. See Simon Lacerous, "Another Book to Cross Off Your List" in *The Pooh Perplex* (New York: E. P. Dutton, 1965), a book of brilliant literary parodies by Frederick C. Crews. In the Lacerous parody, the journal edited by Simon and Trixie Lacerous is called *Thumbscrew*.

2. See *D. H. Lawrence: Novelist* (London: Chatto & Windus,

For Leavis, then, Lawrence belongs among the very great writers. One may find fault with him—Leavis finds "problems" even in *The Rainbow* and *Women in Love*, which he takes to be Lawrence's two indisputably major novels—but one must also acknowledge that no one has made a greater contribution to our civilization or to the art of fiction. Here and there, Leavis concedes, the writing may become a little shrill; *The Plumed Serpent* was perhaps "regrettable"; *The Lost Girl*, though "acute" and full of "insight" yet lacks a "compelling total significance"; and so on. What we must never forget is that Lawrence is the one writer of our time who speaks consistently from a vital moral perspective, whose works minister to life in an altogether healthy way.

Most literate people would now seem to believe that Lawrence *was* a great writer. But it was not always so. T. S. Eliot, for example, did not think Lawrence a great novelist and did what he could to ensure that others would adopt his unfavorable estimation of Lawrence's talents and intelligence. For this deplorable error of judgment Leavis has never really been able to forgive Eliot. Nor has he forgiven members of the Bloomsbury circle for looking down their well-turned noses at Lawrence and making light of him even at his death.[3] In fact, it may be fair to say that Leavis finds so much in Lawrence to love

---

1955), pp. 9–27. Comparable passages may be found in Leavis's second Lawrence book, *Thought, Words, and Creativity* (New York: Oxford, 1976).

3. That Lawrence went out of his way to ridicule and to utterly devastate Bloomsbury—including John Maynard Keynes, Clive Bell, and all their friends—does not give Leavis a moment's unease. For Lawrence was right, after all: Bloomsbury was an awful place fit only for snobs and playboys and everything a la mode. Lawrence's "revenge" on Bloomsbury is contained in such notable works as *St. Mawr* and in substantial sections of *Women in Love*. See Leavis on *St. Mawr* in *D. H. Lawrence: Novelist*.

not only because of the intrinsic merit of the novels and tales but also because of the example presented by his career. Lawrence's novels were banned, or confiscated, or abused; he provoked the contempt of distinguished contemporaries; he died without having received the acclaim subsequent generations would provide. Better yet, he proved—in his lifetime and for a good twenty years later —that the best-placed people are often apt to be narrow-minded, smug, and vicious when at all challenged by something unfamiliar. Leavis's downrightness as a critic early made him unpopular in the Cambridge ruling circles that had little use for Lawrence. No wonder that Leavis should have felt so considerable an identification as the years went by. Though his books were neither banned nor confiscated, Leavis was himself subject to frequent abuse, and though he may not have courted active disfavor, he certainly enjoyed the opportunity to counterattack. Lawrence seemed an ideal ally: he needed a friend and he wasn't around to interfere with the various projects Leavis was busily mounting on his behalf. Had he lived longer, Lawrence might have had to inform his friend that he did not wish to be associated with the likes of Henry James and Joseph Conrad in the ranks of Leavis's Great Tradition. In all, Leavis was fortunate in his selection of a writer who died in 1930 and left behind an enormous body of work in which to discriminate better from best. And while Lawrence has brought out many of the critic's worst tendencies—to categorical overstatement, establishment-baiting, and vacuous life affirmation —he has also given Leavis an authoritative working model and a critical cause. If we feel we understand what Leavis has always intended by judicial criticism, we are confident because the work on Lawrence speaks so clearly of the essential values.

The essential values are not, for Leavis, literary values: this he has stressed again and again. They are values that may be expressed or intimated in works of literature, and they are subject to laws determined by the works in which they are expressed. But they may not be literary values as such. The Eliot who "is not interested in what Pound says, but only in the way he says it," in Leavis's account, does not know what we mean by essential values. To be moved predominantly or exclusively by pure expressive achievement is to prefer, say, Joyce to Lawrence, to prefer "insistent will and ingenuity" to genuine visionary breadth.[4] Lawrence was a great creative writer because he was not afraid to make judgments, because he judged with the fullness of his entire being. When a "positive" character in Lawrence chooses one way instead of another, we feel that the essential values have been brought to bear, even when they have not been explicitly formulated. What matters to Leavis is that the essential values, when properly held, always enable judgments of a positive kind. Lawrence has been a healthy influence because, even when negative judgments seem to focus the interest, they are characteristically accompanied by strong feelings. Where there is genuine conviction and strong emotion, suitable objects are likely to be found for the expression of positive sentiments. If there is much in the world to despise, Lawrence would seem to suggest, there must also be something to inspire affection, or respect.

Leavis does best with Lawrence when he has a text open before him and when he forgets about the general judgment he wishes to enforce. Lawrence was not the entirely sane and healthy fellow Leavis wants him to be, but there are plenty of positive convictions and subtle analyses in his novels for the critic to engage. Does this mean that Leavis is successful only as a New Critic, as

4. See *D. H. Lawrence: Novelist*, p. 27.

an interpreter of texts? Leavis's readings of Lawrence are in no way limited to plodding analyses of images or nimble hunts for life-affirming subtleties. They succeed insofar as they are moved to plot the course of Lawrence's radically unstable and obsessively critical intelligence. Such readings follow the argument embedded in a text with no view toward conclusively extricating it from its context and instating it as a position. Where the readings fail, they are too avid to make Lawrence stand for something that cannot be effectively communicated by the critic outside of his active engagement with the Lawrentian text. That is why Leavis's books on Lawrence, both of them, are least satisfactory in their general opening chapters and in their concluding position statements. Leavis has never been very good at the level of formulaic abstraction. Those who think of him as a culture-prophet in his own right have simply shut their eyes and ears to the shrill and improbable hysteria that characterizes the worst passages of his work on Lawrence. If the essential values are not, for Leavis, literary values, it is nonetheless clear that he cannot effectively communicate his feeling for them apart from his feeling for those literary forms that make them palpable.

In Lawrence there is always an expressed antagonism toward abstraction, particularly toward abstract goodness or ethical devotion. Such sentiments are seen to accompany other generally unhealthy developments in human character. Complacency is likely to be the consequence of abstract addictions, and what Leavis calls "normative aspiration" will then turn into the plain desire to be average, to feel and to think just like everyone else. Lawrence's writing represents a strenuous challenge to the idea of the normal, and if he prided himself on presenting experience in terms of ordinary observation, he surely wished to propose a mode of experience that was anything but ordinary. The literary dimension of this project, such as it was, had to be apprehended not at the level of felicitous expression but at the level of complex organization and narrative tension. Though the fiction has inspired plausible homage directed to its accomplished verbal performance, most of the sustained criticism has followed Leavis in stressing the broader structural elements. Lawrence's expressed antagonism toward abstraction is so persuasive because the antagonism is enacted dramatically within a structure that allows for tensions and counterthrusts. Leavis's primary achievement is to have established, more precisely than anyone else, the principles by which the tensions are organized. In so doing, he has defined the essentially positive element of Lawrentian judgment, and has shown what kind of intelligence is involved in the creative project.

Lawrence's intelligence pits one thought against the other. It doubts what it loves. This is a view that is apt to be questioned by those who have been taught to believe otherwise, but it is accurate and can be proven—insofar as it is possible to prove anything about works of intelligence and imagination—by careful study of the major fiction. Leavis is drawn to Lawrence because his intelligence is fundamentally appealing to him in the way it works, not merely in the finished opinions or positions at which it typically arrives. To state these opinions is to see at once that they have little to do with the qualities that make Lawrence an impressive figure. Leavis notes in Lawrence "an insistent and over-emphatic explicitness" that may prompt one to speak of "jargon" in the language of the novels. Clearly, Lawrence sometimes given to believe in his formulations in a way that betrayed his own better impulses to critical mistrust and scrupulous self-analysis. When he writes of "free proud singleness" and the necessity to "abandon oneself utterly to the moments,"[5] we feel most often that he is mouthing sentiments he cannot properly control, that he is vague and willful where what is wanted is precise articulation or utter awful silence. But the overarching context of the achieved fiction is such that the vague and willful, jargon-ridden sentiments are themselves dramatically challenged within the fictions themselves. Lawrence judges his own formulations as surely as the novels are themselves judged by the Leavis who is so deeply drawn to identify with their visionary purposes. The restless intelligence that sets up a "favored" figure only to expose his radical insufficiency finds an answering and sympathetic respondent in the critic who exalts Lawrence only to demonstrate—whatever his stated intention— how finally limited are the actual benefits of the visionary project. Lawrence was a severe judge of the contemporary universe he inhabited and Leavis's judgments have been known to verge on sour misanthropy. But no serious student of their work will doubt that the judgments represent a strenuous process of enquiry and contain an elaborated dimension of uncertainty that stands in permanent tension with the more confident positions they assert.

Leavis has helped to make *Women in Love* the most admired of Lawrence's novels. Though it is intermittently flawed, though it has been "sincerely" misread by a great many educated readers, it seems to Leavis and to others a great and luminous book that has more to tell us about the way we are than any other novel. The judgment is characteristically definite and unambivalent. It may take a while to arrive at the only sensible conclusion, but arrive you will if you are assiduous and capable. The book is ideally suited not only to Leavis's purposes, but to his talents as a close reader. It is a long novel, and it contains in suspension so many views and patently un-

5. The words are taken from *Women in Love*.

106

acceptable or contradictory "resolutions" that it requires something of a genius to determine which of them are more worthy of attention than others. This, Leavis demonstrates, is not a matter of simple textual analysis. The Lawrentian character may speak with total conviction and passionate urgency a bit of fatuous nonsense, only to emerge a few pages later with something sharp and provocative. A perfectly sensible statement may come to seem foolish and self-serving in the perspective of the novel as a whole, and what appears desperate in the mouth of one character may seem almost persuasive in the mouth of another. Though Leavis can go on and on about Lawrence's commitment to life, about his "incorruptible" integrity and the wondrous perfection of his "art speech," he is really extraordinarily precise in showing us how to distinguish the acceptable from the unacceptable in Lawrence. He shows us, that is to say, not merely what Lawrence wanted us to value but how it is possible to discover for oneself what Lawrence had in mind. In showing us how to make our way through Lawrence, he provides a model of *collaborative* reading, and demonstrates the kind of intelligence he wants us to value in Lawrence. *Women in Love*, whatever its pretensions or recommendations to the contrary, is a novel about intelligence and about the way it arrives at judgments. It enacts in its own way the very process of intelligence it wishes to examine and ultimately to propose. It invites from Leavis a distinguished effort of collaborative intelligence because it is ever so much more than the single thoughts and rejections that are so much a part of the life of its characters. Leavis knows *Women in Love* in the sense that he never tires of following its movements, and is never finally tempted to banish its tensions. In its restless intelligence the novel appeals to what is best in the critic.

Now this is nothing like the intelligence we associate with the so-called liberal imagination, which takes pleasure in moving among impressions and ideas without experiencing any overwhelming pressure to seek resolutions and banish tensions. Such an intelligence is characteristically more urbane and smoothly flowing than the intelligence we associate with Lawrence, and with Leavis. Lawrence wanted very much to achieve a satisfactory and comprehensive resolution in composing *Women in Love*. He wished not merely to end the novel to a burst of applause but to prove something and to change the course of human life. He had much the same desire when he wrote other books, including those—like *The Plumed Serpent*—that were not so well conceived or so carefully executed. The apocalyptic component in Lawrence's nature pressed him to feel that there might be a turning point in the fortunes of the civilization to which he might point the way. We measure his intelligence by coming to appreciate what it cost Lawrence to resist that pressure, how resourceful he had to be to outthink his own salvational propensities. Leavis, too, is drawn by the visionary ultimacies to which Lawrence points, and he too has a great deal to resist in his passionate appropriation of Lawrence. For the liberal imagination, by contrast, there is no ultimacy. Prospective resolutions to enduring conflict are entertained in a spirit of enterprising connoisseurship. Wise men know that making up one's mind is a discipline that one learns to practice sensibly, without investing very much in the conclusions reached. Lawrence and Leavis are, in this sense, neither wise nor urbane. They demand intemperately what they know they aren't about to get. They invite tension and conflict in the spirit of those who believe there must be an end in view, but they resist the various ends generated in the process of pursuit. Their proclamations, whether of apocalyptic fervor (Lawrence) or of hero-worshipping apostleship (Leavis) incur active disapproval because they are so fundamentally at odds with the vital intelligence they subserve. Otherwise we should ignore the frenzied proclamations and turn away from their authors as we do from those who are possessed by a truth to which no one else has access.

Leavis is usually aware of the dangers to which his partisanship exposes him. He knows he will be thought narrow or hysterical. He knows that Lawrence occasionally wrote stupid and indefensible things and that respectably intelligent persons have thought him deliberately cruel and malicious. To identify one's sense of positive good with the vision of such a person is to invite the charge that one is blind to his faults or coldly insensitive in the same degree. Leavis is not always alert to the danger in an immediate way. He can defend Lawrence where defense seems futile, and unnecessary. He can whip himself up into righteous wrath at the enemies of enlightenment (frequently arts council administrators, book reviewers, or distinguished academics) in a way that brings to mind the worst excesses of Lawrence's vituperation. That is why he so desperately needs the Lawrentian text before him. When the words on the page focus his observation, he becomes fully sensitive to the intellectual violence that may be committed in the name of overcoming, spontaneity, individuality, mastery, or any of the other notions Lawrence thought to cultivate. Leavis is so good on *Women in Love* because the novel so clearly mistrusts its own willed conclusions, because it puts one constantly in mind of the terrible resistances built into the fabric of its own unfolding design.

Thus, though Leavis can speak of an "over-emphatic explicitness" in passages of *Women in Love*, of Lawrence's having been "uncertain of the value of what he offers," the novel seems to him—and, consequently, to us—a genuine masterpiece with every prospect of permanently affecting our view of intelligence. Again, the key to Leavis's appreciation is the novel's organization, by means of which central characters and formulated attitudes are, as Leavis says, "exposed to the implicit criticism of the whole creative context." This much, at least, it is possible to confirm and to discuss without revisiting the novel in explicit detail. Rupert Birkin is without doubt Lawrence's spokesman in the novel, the "special representative of Lawrence's conscious and formulated attitudes." As such, he may be said to carry forward in an impressively deliberate way several of the attitudes to which Ursula Brangwen was tending at the end of *The Rainbow,* and with which she struggles as Birkin's consort in *Women in Love.* These attitudes we shall examine, if only briefly, as they bear upon Leavis's sense of essential value. But we must first consider how it is that Lawrence's intelligence so especially manifests itself in arranging for the "implicit criticism" Leavis describes. If Birkin and Ursula may be said to stand for and to articulate the positive values to which Lawrence is attached, why should he have wished to expose them to criticism of any kind? The answer may have a great deal to do with the man Lawrence was and the experience he had in part to overcome in order to do his work. But that is not where our interest must lie.[6] Though Lawrence invested a great deal of himself in Birkin, he was not, finally, as interested in the fate of the individual character as in particular representative qualities. The novelist sees what Birkin himself can be made intermittently to see: that the powerful "mental consciousness" Birkin embodies is susceptible to perversion. And this perversion, Leavis insists, is not likely only to be the work of triflers and "outsiders"; it is an

6. The personal "victory" of Lawrence is interestingly discussed by Roger Sale in the Lawrence chapter of his *Modern Heroism* (Berkeley: University of California Press, 1973).

ever-present potentiality within Birkin's experience of himself. Lawrence deliberately constructs the novel to indicate that, whatever Birkin's potential for positive good, there are possibilities to which he may not be fully equal. These "negative" possibilities are at once the dark side of his own character and the embodied "reality" of other types whose fate Birkin cannot affect.

Lawrence's intelligence is very much the issue in a consideration of organizational principles. *Women in Love* has produced a great many conflicting testimonies and critiques. It seems not to settle anything in a decisive way, despite the many claims Birkin especially is prone to make. If Birkin is "placed," as Leavis says, it is surely not possible to follow him to that "place." The novel refuses the prophetic mission it takes upon itself. This it does by centering so much of its attention on Gerald Crich, precisely when the reader might have thought him incidental to larger developments in Birkin and Ursula. Leavis rightly reminds us that "no separation. . . . can really be made: the total drama is a closely organized whole, and the significance depends upon (among other things) the interplay between the two halves of the quartet" (Birkin-Ursula, Gerald-Gudrun). It is the interplay that recommends authorial intelligence, for it allows us progressively to understand that Birkin cannot finally get to Gerald, cannot finally take over, control, or repudiate what he represents. So involved is Birkin and the very consciousness he embodies in the perversion that is Gerald Crich that Birkin can at best be made to withdraw from the conflict to find a kind of private repose with Ursula. Lawrence's intelligence is more than the insight that Birkin, like the novelist himself, is radically flawed. He makes us feel that thought is itself unstable and susceptible to unpredictable motions. This is not a theory but a demonstration of what it is like to be fully conscious and to propose as objects of reflection what can never be satisfactorily encompassed. If, for Leavis, Lawrence is the great writer of the age, the achievement of *Women in Love* is to have proposed a great fulfillment which, though denied, is vindicated by the intelligence that has worked to imagine it.

Gerald Crich is not alone in suggesting, by his very presence and by the terrible extremity of his awful fate, that Birkin cannot hope to accomplish a general prophecy. Ursula herself, as Birkin's cherished mate, assumes part of the responsibility for the "implicit critique" the novel may be said to administer. It is she who argues with Birkin, who taunts him and brings to bear the kind of ironic scrutiny to which the prophetic fury must succumb if it is not to burn itself out in wasteful seizures. Though she goes in for the "full mystic knowledge" Lawrence likes to claim as the special province of his favorite couple, she has a firmer commitment than Birkin to the proximate and the possible, and a healthy distrust of the "something diffuse and generalized" to which he is routinely tempted. She is not the entirely impressive character Lawrence developed in the concluding pages of *The Rainbow*, but her capacity for skeptical valuation is an entirely necessary component of a book that has Birkin so much at its center. Frank Kermode, in his book on Lawrence, is surely right when he insists that the novelist "was not deficient in common sense, even in intellectual and spiritual prudence," whatever his works' "desperate religious plunges into an unknown Lawrence so much wanted."[7] The prudence, which has nothing to do with a queasy timidity, in *Women in Love* is largely represented by Ursula. To her we owe our sense that Lawrence is fully sensitive to the limitations intrinsic to Birkin's mental consciousness. In surrounding Birkin as he does, in organizing the novel so consistently to administer its im-

7. See Frank Kermode, *D. H. Lawrence* (New York: Viking, 1973), pp. 65–66.

plicit critique, Lawrence demonstrates the central truth to which Leavis regularly points: that intelligence is critical intelligence and that works of art bear witness to this fact better than any other mode of expression.

The critical thinking that is so much a part of the project of *Women in Love* has a whole range of highly charged attitudes to contend with. These attitudes are developed, challenged, and reformulated in waves of alternating intensity that beat steadily through the rhythms of the novel. Throughout, one has the sense that a rhythm is established only to be brought to a halt and displaced by something that, though it remembers what has gone before, is impatient to press ahead. Recurrences are obvious—Lawrence repeats with obsessional insistence his primary value–terms—but every value–term seems finally unstable and unreliable in the way that it is fiercely recast in one passage after another. Perhaps there is something in the attitudes themselves that requires perpetual revision and displacement. No one will imagine that Lawrence was fascinated, or tormented, by the *mot juste in the spirit of a Flaubert*. He was less interested in getting something right than in exercising his intelligence in a way that seemed suitable to his own urgent needs. Those needs are expressed, implicitly at least, in the formulated attitudes. Central to these is the view, as put by Leavis, that "will and 'idea', controlling from above, have usurped the direction" of our civilization; more, "the smooth-running of an almost inconceivably intricate interlocking of mechanisms has become the supreme end." If this is the case, Leavis goes on to argue, it is not in "flight from intelligence and responsibility" that Lawrence thought to find a way out.[8] *More* responsibility and *better* intelligence were to be recommended, not the "cult of the primitive" or the sort of bloody nonsense casually attributed to Lawrence by careless readers.

8. See the discussion in *D. H. Lawrence: Novelist*, pp. 166–69.

To propose attitudes in a summary way is inevitably to do them an injustice, of course, and it is not the business of this study to give a detailed account of Lawrence's attitudes. Leavis has himself spoken of "my clumsy commentary"[9] in trying to account for the disparity between attitudes expressed in summary and the same attitudes evoked in a finished work of fiction. If Lawrence's thought is the completed work itself in all its complex organization, then no summary may be said to do the job adequately. With other writers it may be possible to isolate fragments of completed texts and to make them yield what would seem to be representative statements of central attitudes. To say that Lawrence resists that kind of interpretative procedure is to indicate how difficult is Leavis's object: to evoke the living element in Lawrence's fiction in a way that will engage essential values without pretending to have isolated them in a precise or fully satisfactory way. To suggest that the basic attitudes may themselves require revision and displacement is a way of saying that they do not seem entirely to belong to Lawrence. The attitudes shift and reshape themselves in response to an energy and pressure that the novelist may be said to focus, though they are not his alone, any more than a single attitude may be said to speak for him unequivocally. Lawrence's intelligence so appeals to Leavis because, at its best, it has the "impersonal wholeness" that characterizes genuine thought.

We may bring these related notions together by considering Lawrence's impersonality as a function of the special intensity with which his major characters move, and with which he directs and follows their movements. Leavis speaks of it in religious terms and would seem to have some reason for doing so: "What, in fact, strikes us as religious is the intensity with which his men and

9. See the chapter on "The Captain's Doll" in the second Lawrence book, *Thought, Words, and Creativity*, esp. p. 121.

women, hearkening to their deepest needs and prompt-
ings as they seek 'fulfilment' in marriage, know that they
'do not belong to themselves', but are responsible to
something that, in transcending the individual, transcends
love and sex too."[10] That is to say, Lawrence will identify
with the aspirations of characters only in the degree that
they "are responsible to" that "something" that transcends their individual projects as men and women. The
intensity they feel is a consequence of their ambition to
make contact with a truth to which they are never perfectly equal. Call it what we will, that truth is a judgment
whose operant terms have nothing to do with particular
needs or demands. The judgment does not require that we
deny need or cease to make demands, only that we see
to it that they fall under the determining sway of something greater. Leavis speaks of the something greater in
terms of the religious intensity required to apprehend it;
he knows that it is elusive and will yield intermittently
only to those who are reverently attentive. The something greater is a judgment we are asked to pass, perpetu-
ally, upon ourselves and upon those who come before us.
If we do not belong to ourselves, if our attitudes are constantly in process of reformulation, that is because we
have made ourselves subject to that process of judgment
which is ceaselessly self-renewing. Those who refuse to
be responsible to the something greater may achieve
comfortable lives, but they will be spiritually dead.

The impersonality of which Leavis speaks, here (in
the Lawrentian context) as elsewhere, is so crucial because it describes the discipline of thought to which he
is committed. But the notion is not easily defined. It is
in a way what we mean when we speak of characters not
belonging to themselves, of the writer's attitudes not
belonging to him in a definitive or narrow way. But this
is not all. When Leavis finds in Lawrence a responsiveness

10. *D. H. Lawrence: Novelist*, p. 111.

115

to values "transcending the individual," he does not discount the individual or imply that judgment is not a matter of individual responsibility. The impersonality is the condition of individual judgment, not its negation. Values transcending the individual, properly—even if imperfectly—apprehended, enable the sense of identity in the only way that can possibly matter. Consider: "Will . . . . [in the positive sense] represents, not the mental 'idea' stubbornly seeking to impose itself on the spontaneous life, but the wholeness of the being . . . . in which the conscious mind does truly serve the life that transcends it."[11] That is to say, when we properly execute an act of will, when we make a judgment and pursue what it recommends, we consider implicitly more than the object of our desire and the dominant idea that accompanies or rationalizes our desiring. The "mental 'idea'" we have may represent only a passing fancy or a stubborn notion that one object ought to be preferred to another—an inherited notion, perhaps, or a notion associated with a sensation we experience when we will what we think we're expected to will. Leavis makes of judgment a *positive* thing when it issues from a "wholeness of the being . . . in which the conscious mind does truly serve the life that transcends it." We are genuinely in touch with the sources of a judgment and may therefore be prepared to stand by it only when we feel that the judgment bears witness to a truth that is greater than anything designated in the immediate testimony. The judgment is a positive act of will in the sense that it affirms what we truly know ourselves to be and the values by which our being may be said largely to abide. The life that transcends our being is the truth we honor when we say that we are genuinely suited to do this rather than that, or that our judgment is required to take one direction rather than another. The will is healthy when it counsels us, implicitly, to under-

11. Ibid., p. 84.

116

take what is truly ours to do, when it is responsive to general laws the conscious mind may not entirely make up by itself. The judgment is life enhancing when the individual is responsive to the truth he has learned to respect by attending in a disciplined way to the laws of his own nature. The individual being takes its proper shape and direction by submitting its various designs to the *impersonal* necessity we come to ratify in every faculty we can summon.

Lawrence was not, then, a strident prophet of apocalypse but a great critic of our civilization who diagnosed the spiritual sickness of the age as a disease of will, a perversion of mental consciousness. For Leavis, the diagnosis is especially telling as it reflects upon our collective inability to distinguish one thing from another, our general refusal to adduce firm values and standards in arriving at judgments, which we take to be expressive of merely individual predilection and personal experience. As we believe we have the power to believe or to feel what we wish, simply by proposing particular objects as suitable and various egalitarian social goals as therapeutic, so we believe that no one ought to be able to make judgments that will seem authoritative or binding to anyone else. If, as the saying has it, everything is "relative," it may be said to seem so because we believe that we can turn all things to our purposes, that nothing can resist our will. For Lawrence, and for Leavis, an age of "social engineering" was a disaster in the degree that it encouraged people to feel that they were responsible largely to their needs and to the calculations that would satisfy them. To those personal needs Leavis's Lawrence did not oppose an irrationalist doctrine but an embodied discipline of thought that would subject personal calculation to the scrutiny of an impersonal judgment. We know that Lawrence could, in his lesser work, whip himself up into a sort of heightened irrationalist prophetism bordering on frenzy, but that is not the Lawrence that Leavis chiefly admires. Nor does he close his eyes to the Lawrence who could be tempted to identify too closely with the solutions proposed by one novelistic character or another. The novelist Leavis admires demonstrates substantial human weakness, but his best work is proof against that weakness.

Among the fictions Leavis admires especially are the novellas and short tales, several of which allow him to show the critical values Lawrence affirmed. The critic is especially good on works like *St. Mawr*, where the engagement with positive values doesn't unduly tempt Lawrence to diagrammatic resolutions such as those we find notably in more ambitious books like *The Plumed Serpent* and *Aaron's Rod*.[12] Leavis is also impressive on an early, little noticed tale called "The Daughter of the Vicar," which he discusses under the heading, "Lawrence and Class."[13] But it is not the issue of class that most engages our interest in Leavis's study, though he does conclusively refute the silly contention that Lawrence was class-bound and superior in damaging ways. What we mostly admire is Leavis's examination of judgment in Lawrence, of the relation between a contemptuous or absolutely dismissive judgment and the quality of thought that may be said to inform it. For Leavis shows us that in "The Daughter of the Vicar" there is an enacted judgment that does truly represent the full being and impersonal discipline of its protagonist. The story, though it richly develops its materials, is not so complex or tentative as to require detailed commentary here, but it may be useful to stress Leavis's key observations: 1) There is an "essential tenderness" in Lawrence that is a vital com-

12. See Eliseo Vivas's argument with Leavis on the issues of value and resolution in *Aaron's Rod*: in Vivas's *D. H. Lawrence: The Failure and The Triumph of Art* (Evanston: Northwestern University Press, 1960), pp. 30–35.

13. Chapter 2 of *D. H. Lawrence: Novelist*, pp. 73–95.

ponent of his ability to move us favorably even when his criticism is harsh and negative. His central character, Louisa, demonstrates a positive capacity for reverence even though she can pronounce a prospective suitor "a little abortion." 2) The right to judge is validated by an accompanying capacity to attend to ordinary realities with a sense of their necessary relation to oneself. Louisa doesn't stand apart from the judgments she enacts, but is directed by the "reality of the 'real' things that she invokes against the 'abstract goodness' " to which others are attracted. 3) Positive judgments inevitably complete themselves in a process of "conscious and deliberate" thought. Louisa's feelings have "her mind's full 'connivance,' " and the fact that "she is an educated woman has its essential part in her significance." Though Louisa might well have arrived at a particular dismissive judgment without having been an educated person, the *quality* of the judgment here is a function of the scrupulous thought and refined feeling that support and direct the character's impulse.

Leavis's feeling for Lawrence, for what is best in the writing, doesn't always ensure that he will succeed in persuading others. Though his account of thought and judgment in "The Daughter of the Vicar" is a powerful and convincing argument, the defense of other fictions may seem ill conceived. Leavis has staked a good deal on a novella entitled "The Captain's Doll," to which he devotes full-length chapters in both books on Lawrence.[14] Nothing in either volume seems to me so peculiar as the compulsion to make a case for a tale that, as Frank Kermode puts it, is so patently "too much for its author."[15] If the materials were too much for Lawrence, they were too much as well for Leavis, who would seem to have

14. Chapter 5 of *D. H. Lawrence: Novelist*, and Chapter 4 of *Thought, Words, and Creativity*.
15. Kermode's remarks appear in *D. H. Lawrence*, p. 102.

mistaken ambiguity bordering on sheer confusion for subtlety of insight. Did his ability to read fail Leavis suddenly, or is there something in "The Captain's Doll" that might disorient any reader? The novella is unusual in a variety of ways, but in one particular especially: though it is built around a concrete image and has several reliable counters by which to measure Lawrence's support of different attitudes, it is finally elusive even on major issues. To speak of an implicit critique offered by one particular in the tale to another is to overlook the quality of sheer *inarticulate* incomprehension we are asked to accept. Leavis speaks of Lawrence's "unamenableness to orderly exposition" as if this were a creative principle no one would be so mindless as to deplore. And, in fact, it is not orderly exposition that we miss in the tale, but the willingness to engage precisely what is meant by its central value–terms: love, individuality, life. Clearly Leavis wants to use the tale because it represents a great challenge. It is an ambitious work on a small scale and resists simple interpretative commentary almost on principle. As such, it tempts the critic who is bent on demonstrating "that the most important kind of thought is decidedly *not* philosophical,"[16] and is therefore inimical "to the ethos of *la clarte* and 'clear and distinct ideas.' "

For a critic of Leavis's general disposition to make a case for a work like "The Captain's Doll" is necessarily to go against the grain of better instincts. He forces readings in a way that can only disappoint and confuse admirers. Assiduous to prove that Lawrence will not countenance "limpness" or "weak irresolution," he is forced to cite passages that are nothing if not irresolute and betray a quality of thought that leaves much to be desired. He is impressed by the seriousness and intellectual profundity of a male protagonist who cannot communicate his primary feelings to the woman he loves and whose ref-

16. *Thought, Words, and Creativity*, pp. 92, 97.

utations are composed of formulations like "I didn't say that" and "No-no- that's hardly the way to look at it." We are to be taken with Lawrence's Captain because we may be sure that his statements "mean something— something basically important—to him, and that we shall in due course appreciate the meaning."[17] Though we never have reason to feel that the Captain has made himself clear, or that Lawrence has been able to understand his meanings any better than we can, Leavis supposes that we can be satisfied by the aura of potent mystery and male sufficiency the novelist weaves around his creations. In this spirit Leavis succumbs to the worst excesses of the Lawrentian life-mystique and produces his own brew of ponderous banality, to wit:

> The Captain's mystery is so potent because the life in him flows with unusual freedom from the source or well-head, so that he has the responsibility of one who is exquisitely sensitive to the unknown, and, being in delicate touch with the dark pregnancy, is capable of wonder —and of growth; that is, new livingness, which issues from the as yet unknown. When Hannele is informed by his presence she feels herself alive to the cosmos.

There is no need to pursue this further. Simply, Leavis ceases to function as a critic when he gives himself over to Lawrence in a spirit of trusting discipleship. Though the second study on "The Captain's Doll" superficially resembles the textual approach we have come to associate with Leavis, it betrays everywhere an impulse to trust not so much the tale as the teller. Were Leavis more skeptical about Lawrence, more willing to think him capable of weak irresolution or stubborn blundering, he would see more clearly the terrible flaws in the very passages he cites. Fortunately, Leavis's instincts are generally reliable where Lawrence is concerned, and he writes memorably of fictions that deserve his careful scrutiny. He finds in

17. Ibid., pp. 102–3.

Lawrence a quality of thought that is often equal to the demands he places upon it. So strong is the identification produced by the critical transaction, in fact, that Leavis's failure with "The Captain's Doll" might almost be termed a failure of self-knowledge or self-criticism. As such, it remains unfortunate, and eminently forgivable.

Leavis's work on Lawrence does, then, indicate the various strengths and dangers of judicial criticism. Its distinction lies in a scrupulous demonstration of the critical thinking necessary for any kind of positive judgment. Also, it provides a model of collaborative reading whereby the original text is engaged in a spirit consistent with, though not identical to, the original authorial project. The impersonality of the primary text is answered by a disciplined impersonality in the collaborative commentary, so that values and standards beyond anything deliberately aimed at by author or critic are brought into play. The judicial project fails when the overarching value judgment obstructs the local discriminations upon which critical thinking absolutely depends. If Leavis was a great critic, his achievement may be said to testify to the resistance he gave to his own potentially immobilizing judgments. That resistance—whatever the occasions on which it has broken down—is exemplary, and ought not to be overlooked even by those who believe only in the virtues of politeness and composure. We may say of Leavis, as we say of Lawrence, that the activity of thought to which they devoted their lives allowed them often to reach beyond what they felt or imagined in their weaker moments. In both, it is *disciplined* instinct that may be said to have been the determining factor. Our capacity to judge them is a capacity we have learned, in part, from them both. To think of Leavis in this way, alongside of Lawrence, is to remark again the power and urgency generated by criticism at its best.